D0468012

CREATIVE
Christmas Cakes

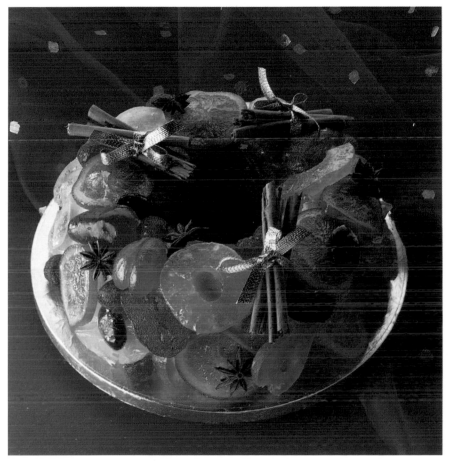

Joanna Farrow

MEREHURST

First published in 1995 by Merehurst Limited
Ferry House, 51-57 Lacy Road, Putney, London SW15 1PR
Copyright © 1995 Merehurst Limited
ISBN 1 85391 484 3

All rights reserved. No part of this publication may be reproduced, stored
in a retrieval system, or transmitted in any form or by any means,
electronic, mechanical, photocopying, recording or otherwise, without the
prior written permission of the copyright owner.

A catalogue record for this book is available from the British Library.

Edited by Donna Wood
Designed by Maggie Aldred
Photography by James Duncan
Illustrations by King & King Design Associates
Typesetting by Peter A. Lovell
Colour separation by Global Colour, Malaysia
Printed in Italy by G. Canale & C SpA

Contents

Basic Cake Recipes

RICH FRUIT CAKE

For ingredients, tin sizes and baking times, see the chart below. Rich fruit cake stores well for several months in a cool, dry place. Leave the lining paper on and wrap in plenty of foil. If liked, drizzle the cake with brandy before storing.

1. Preheat the oven to 140°C (275°F/Gas1). Grease and line the required tin.
2. Cream together the butter or margarine and sugar. Lightly beat the eggs and gradually beat into the creamed mixture, adding a little of the flour to prevent curdling. Sift together the remaining flour with the spice and fold into the mixture.
3. Gradually add the mixed fruit, cherries and nuts, stirring until evenly blended. Turn into the prepared tin and level the surface.
4. Bake in the oven for the time stated in the chart. (The time will vary considerably, depending on the type of oven). Use the chart as a guide and test towards the end of the stated time. A skewer inserted into the centre should come out clean. Leave the cake to cool in the tin, then turn out, wrap and store.

LIGHT FRUIT CAKE

This is ideal for those who find rich fruit cake a little too heavy. It still contains plenty of fruit but has a more spongy texture. Make up to 1 month before Christmas and store, wrapped in its lining paper, in plenty of foil. For ingredients, tin sizes and baking times, see the chart opposite.

1. Preheat the oven to 140°C (275°F/Gas 1). Grease and line the required tin.
2. Place the mixed dried fruit, peel and apricots in

RICH FRUIT CAKE QUANTITIES CHART

Round tin	18cm (7 in)	20cm (8 in)	23cm (9 in)	25cm (10 in)	28cm (11 in)
Square tin	15cm (6 in)	18cm (7 in)	20cm (8 in)	23cm (9 in)	25cm (10 in)
Butter or margarine, softened	155g (5 oz)	200g (6½ oz)	280g (9 oz)	410g (13 oz)	470g (15 oz)
Dark muscovado sugar	155g (5 oz)	200g (6½ oz)	280g (9 oz)	410g (13 oz)	470g (15 oz)
Plain flour	185g (6 oz)	250g (8 oz)	375g (12 oz)	500g (1 lb)	625g (1¼ lb)
Ground mixed spice	1 tsp	1½ tsp	2 tsp	1 tbsp	4 tsp
Eggs	3	3	4	6	8
Mixed dried fruit	625g (1¼ lb)	875g (1¾ lb)	1.1kg (2¼ lb)	1.5kg (3 lb)	1.8kg (3¾ lb)
Glacé cherries, chopped	60g (2 oz)	90g (3 oz)	100g (3½ oz)	155g (5 oz)	250g (8 oz)
Chopped almonds	30g (1 oz)	45g (1½ oz)	60g (2 oz)	90g (3 oz)	125g (4 oz)
Baking time	2-2¼ hours	3-3¼ hours	3½-3¾ hours	4 hours	4½-4¾ hours

LIGHT FRUIT CAKE QUANTITIES CHART

Round tin	18cm (7 in)	20cm (8 in)	23cm (9 in)	25cm (10 in)	28cm (11 in)
Square tin	15cm (6 in)	18cm (7 in)	20cm (8 in)	23cm (9 in)	25cm (10 in)
Mixed dried fruit	440g (14 oz)	500g (1 lb)	750g (1½ lb)	1kg (2 lb)	1.25kg (2½ lb)
Mixed peel	30g (1 oz)	30g (1 oz)	60g (2 oz)	90g (3 oz)	125g (4 oz)
Dried apricots, chopped	60g (2 oz)	125g (4 oz)	185g (6 oz)	250g (8 oz)	315g (10 oz)
Brandy	2 tbsp	2 tbsp	3 tbsp	3 tbsp	4 tbsp
Butter or margarine, softened	250g (8 oz)	315g (10 oz)	440g (14 oz)	525g (1lb 1oz)	625g (1¼ lb)
Light muscovado sugar	250g (8 oz)	315g (10 oz)	440g (14 oz)	525g (1lb 1oz)	625g (1¼ lb)
Eggs	4	4	5	6	7
Plain flour	315g (10 oz)	375g (12 oz)	500g (1 lb)	625g (1¼ lb)	750g (1½ lb)
Ground mixed spice	1½ tsp	2 tsp	1 tbsp	4 tsp	5 tsp
Baking time	2-2¼ hours	3-3¼ hours	3½-3¾ hours	4 hours	4½-4¾ hours

a bowl. Add the brandy and leave for 2-3 hours.
3. Cream together the butter or margarine and sugar. Lightly beat the eggs and gradually add to the creamed mixture, adding a little of the flour to prevent curdling. Sift together the remaining flour and spice and fold into the mixture.
4. Gradually add the fruit mixture and stir until evenly combined. Turn into the prepared tin and make a deep depression in the centre. Bake in the oven for the time stated in the chart or until a skewer, inserted into the centre, comes out clean. Leave to cool in the tin. Wrap and store.

LINING TINS

For a round tin, place the tin on a piece of greaseproof paper and draw around it, then cut out just inside the line. Cut a strip of paper that is as long as the circumference of the tin and 2.5cm (1 in) deeper. Make a 2.5cm (1 in) fold along one long edge of the strip and snip the folded portion from the edge to the fold at 2.5cm (1 in) intervals. Position the strip around the inside of the greased tin with the snipped edge flat on the base. Place the paper in the base, then grease the paper.

▲ *Lining the sides of a round tin.*

For a square tin, use the same method as for a round tin, although the folded portion will only need snipping in the corners.
For a star-shaped tin, draw and cut around the tin as for a round tin. For the sides, cut strips as before, then snip into the points of the star.
For a ring tin, place the tin on a piece of greaseproof paper and draw around the inside and outside edge of the ring. Cut out the paper ring and press into the base of the greased ring tin. Line the sides with rectangles of paper, generously snipping the paper so that it fits the curves.

APRICOT GLAZE

This is used to moisten the surface of the cake and secure the marzipan (almond paste) to it. Put the apricot jam into a saucepan (see chosen recipe for amount required), adding 5ml (1 tsp) water for each 15ml (1 tbsp) of jam. Heat gently until the jam has melted, then press the mixture through a sieve to remove any pieces.

MARZIPAN (ALMOND PASTE)

Before covering a cake with sugarpaste or royal icing, it is important to create a good, smooth base. This is done by applying a covering of marzipan, now readily available in both super-markets and cake-decorating shops. Before covering, trim the cake to the shape required (see chosen recipe) and fill any small holes or gaps with marzipan. Brush with apricot glaze.

To cover a cake with marzipan (almond paste)

1. Lightly knead the marzipan to soften it. Roll out two-thirds on a surface dusted with icing (confectioner's) sugar to a round or square 5cm (2 in) larger than the diameter of the cake.
2. Place the marzipan on a sheet of greaseproof paper. Invert the cake onto it and press the excess marzipan into the gap left between the cake and the marzipan. Using a sharp knife, cut off the excess. Invert the cake onto the board and remove

the greaseproof paper from the top of the cake.
3. To cover the sides of a round cake, measure the circumference of the cake with a piece of string. Roll out the remaining marzipan to a strip slightly longer than the string and deeper than the cake. Using the string as a guide, cut the strip to the exact circumference of the cake, and then to the exact depth. Roll up the marzipan and unroll around the sides of the cake.
4. Lightly smooth the marzipan around the join and top edge of the cake. Use the same method to cover a square cake, but use four strips of marzipan each the exact measurement of the cake sides.

▲ Invert the cake onto the marzipan, press marzipan into the gap, then cut off the excess.

◀ To cover the sides, cut a strip of marzipan to size, roll it up, then unroll round the cake.

Icing Recipes

SUGARPASTE

You can use either bought or homemade sugarpaste for the cakes in this book. Bought sugarpaste has a similar taste to homemade and is slightly easier to work with. If you are making several cakes, it is worth buying ready-coloured sugarpaste. Strong colours such as red, blue, green and black are particularly good and save you the trouble of kneading in colour. Supermarket sugarpastes vary slightly in quality. Some are very soft and become easier to manage if you work in a little icing (confectioner's) sugar before using. Both homemade and bought sugarpaste should be wrapped tightly in clingfilm (plastic wrap) when not in use as they quickly develop a dry crust. Store in a cool, dry place. Check 'best before' dates on bought sugarpastes. The homemade version will keep for up to 1 week.

Makes 500g (1 lb)

1 egg white · 30 ml (2 tbsp) liquid glucose (available from chemists) · approximately 500g (1 lb) icing (confectioner's) sugar · icing (confectioner's) sugar for dusting

1. Put the egg white and liquid glucose in a bowl. Gradually beat in the icing sugar until the mixture becomes too stiff to stir.
2. Turn it out onto a surface heavily dusted with more icing sugar and knead until it forms a stiff, smooth paste. Wrap in several layers of clingfilm (plastic wrap) until ready to use.

Tips

● If homemade sugarpaste is sticky when rolled, work in more icing (confectioner's) sugar. If too dry and crumbly, work in a little water.
● Most recipes list icing (confectioner's) sugar and cornflour (cornstarch) for dusting.

Icing sugar should be used for rolling and applying marzipan and sugarpaste; cornflour only for smoothing sugarpaste and decorations.

To cover a cake with sugarpaste

1. Lightly knead the required amount of sugarpaste on a surface dusted with icing (confectioner's) sugar. Roll out the paste to a round or square a good 7.5cm (3 in) larger than the diameter of the cake. Lift the sugarpaste on a rolling pin and lay it over the top of the cake.
2. Dust the palms of the hands lightly with cornflour (cornstarch) and smooth the sugarpaste over the top and down the sides of the cake, easing it gently to fit around the sides of the cake.
3. Trim off any excess paste around the base of the cake. For the most professional results use an icing smoother, a flat-sided tool available from cake-decorating shops. Work it in a circular action over the cake, for a beautifully flat surface.

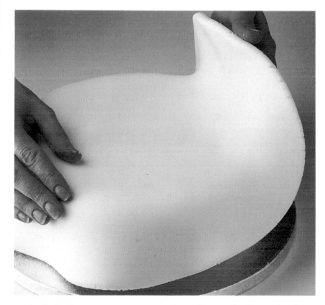

▲ *Lift the sugarpaste onto the cake with the aid of a rolling pin, then smooth into place with the hands.*

Colouring sugarpaste

Lightly knead the sugarpaste on a surface dusted with icing (confectioner's) sugar. Using a cocktail stick (toothpick) dot the paste with colour. Gradually knead it into the paste until evenly coloured, adding more if necessary.

Tip

● Partially kneading in colour gives a streaked, marbled appearance, which can be effective.

ROYAL ICING

Royal icing can be applied to a cake in a smooth 'flat-iced' layer, or, more traditionally on Christmas cakes, as peaked 'snow.' This is particularly easy to do, and does not require the patience, skill and equipment of flat icing. In this book smaller quantities of royal icing are also used for piping, spreading and making decorative run-outs. The quantities below are sufficient for most decorative work.

Makes 250g (8 oz)

1 egg white · 250g (8 oz) icing (confectioner's) sugar, sifted

1. Lightly whisk the egg white in a bowl. Gradually beat in the icing sugar, beating well after each addition until the icing forms soft peaks.
2. Cover the surface of the icing with clingfilm (plastic wrap), then a damp cloth and further clingfilm (plastic wrap) to prevent a crust forming. Well sealed, the royal icing will store in a cool place for several days.

Covering a cake with peaked royal icing

1. Using a palette knife, spread the top and sides of the marzipan-covered cake with royal icing, repeatedly smoothing the knife over the icing until covered in an even layer.
2. Clean the palette knife. Press the palette knife flat onto the icing, then pull away sharply to form a peak. Repeat all over the cake. (See *Fruited 'Snow' Cake,* page 16).

Tips

● Royal icing firms up slightly during storage. Before use beat well to soften, adding a little water or beaten egg white if necessary. For spreading and peaking, royal icing should be softly peaking.
● When piping, remember that the smaller the tube, the thinner the consistency of the icing must be. If you find piping fine lines hard work, the icing probably needs thinning down a little.

▶ To colour sugarpaste, add dots of colouring with a cocktail stick then knead until evenly mixed.

ROYAL ICING TECHNIQUES

Making a paper piping bag

Homemade paper piping bags are far easier to use than bought ones as they are less bulky and can simply be discarded after use. It is worth making several at a time so you always have some at the ready.

1. Cut a 25cm (10 in) square of greaseproof paper, then cut the square in half diagonally to make two triangles. Holding one triangle with its longest side away from you, fold the right-hand point over to meet the bottom point, curling the paper to shape a cone.

2. Fold the left-hand point over the cone and bring all three points together. Fold over several times to secure the bag.

3. Cut 1cm (½ in) off the tip if fitting a piping tube (tip), or snip off the merest tip if piping without a tube (tip).

▲ *Hold the paper triangle with its longest side away from you, then fold the side points over.*

▶ *Once you have the cone shape, fold over several times to secure the bag tightly.*

ROYAL ICING QUANTITIES CHART

Use this chart as a guide for covering a marzipan-covered cake with peaked icing.

Round cake	18cm (7 in)	20cm (8 in)	23cm (9 in)	25cm (10 in)	28cm (11 in)
Square cake	15cm (6 in)	18cm (7 in)	20cm (8 in)	23cm (9 in)	25cm (10 in)
Royal icing quantities	2 egg whites	3 egg whites	4 egg whites	5 egg whites	6 egg whites

Making royal-iced runouts

The *Winter Wonderland* and *Santa Comes To Town* cakes are finished with iced runouts which are piped onto paper, left to harden and then carefully transferred to the cake. This technique can be used equally well using your own designs such as Christmas stockings, stars, candles and other festive shapes, traced from cards, books or drawn by hand. Avoid making them too complicated.

1. Trace the chosen design onto greaseproof or non-stick parchment paper. Place the traced design under a sheet of non-stick parchment paper. Using a little royal icing in a piping bag fitted with a fine or medium writing tube (tip), pipe over the outline.

2. Thin a little more royal icing with beaten egg white or water until it becomes completely level when left to settle in the bowl for 10 seconds. Place in a paper piping bag and snip off 3mm (⅛ in) from the tip. Gradually fill the outline with the icing, easing around the edges and into corners with the tip of a cocktail stick (toothpick).

3. Leave for about 48 hours until completely hardened, then carefully peel the paper away from the icing. If liked, the runout can be painted with diluted food colourings.

▲ *Place your traced design beneath a sheet of non-stick parchment. Pipe over the outline.*

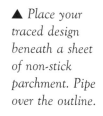

◀ *Fill in the outline with thinned-down royal icing, easing it into the corners with a cocktail stick.*

Basic Techniques

Covering a cakeboard with sugarpaste

This gives a professional-looking finish to a smart or novelty cake.

1. Lightly dampen the surface of the cakeboard. Thinly roll white or coloured sugarpaste to a curved strip, slightly wider than the board area to be covered. Trim the inner edge of the strip with a knife.

2. Lift the strip around the cake so that the trimmed edge rests against the side of the cake. Smooth out the icing using hands dusted with cornflour (cornstarch), then trim off the excess around the edges. On larger cakes it is easier to cover the board in two sections.

Cutting around templates

Rolled sugarpaste, shaped and left to harden, makes effective three-dimensional designs, particularly on novelty cakes. Make them well in advance so they have ample time to harden.

1. Roll out the sugarpaste on a surface lightly dusted with cornflour (cornstarch) to 3mm (⅛ in) thickness, or as stated in the chosen recipe.

2. Lay the cut-out template over the icing and cut around it with a small, sharp knife. Carefully transfer to a sheet of greaseproof or non-stick parchment and leave to harden. (For large templates, lay the icing on the paper before cutting out, as the shape might become distorted if transferred afterwards).

▲ *Lay the template over the sugarpaste and, keeping it very still, cut around it with a sharp knife.*

Making holly leaves

Cut-out holly leaves make an effective decoration on a simple 'snow'-covered cake, or as part of a more involved decoration. Bought holly cutters come in various sizes but the most realistic looking leaves are made using the tip of a piping tube (tip).

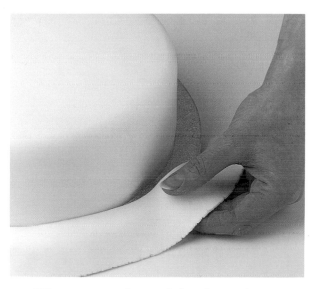

▲ *When covering a large cakeboard it is often easier to apply the sugarpaste in two sections.*

▲ *Cut out semi-circles from the edge of the holly leaf with the wide end of a writing tube (tip).*

1. Thinly roll a little green sugarpaste on a surface dusted with cornflour (cornstarch). Cut out a rough leaf shape about 7.5cm (3 in) long and 4cm (1½ in) wide. Using the wide end of a writing tube (tip) dipped in cornflour, cut out semi-circles from around the shape to create holly leaves.
2. Lightly mark veins with the tip of a knife. Transfer to a sheet of crumpled foil and leave for at least 24 hours.

Tip

● Secure the holly leaves to the cake with a dot of royal icing, propping them up with balls of foil or absorbent kitchen paper until set in position. Add tiny balls of red icing for berries.

Painting sugarpaste

This is best done when the sugarpaste has hardened as you can gently rest your hand against the cake without denting the surface. Freehand painting can be applied directly to the cake. Simpler designs can be made by impressing festive shapes onto soft sugarpaste then filling in with colour once the icing has hardened. Use a size of brush appropriate to the area to be covered.
1. Dilute the chosen food colouring with water to

▲ *Impress the soft sugarpaste with shapes. Leave to harden before filling the outline with colour.*

give the required density. (Test on a little spare icing or white paper first).

2. Use light brush strokes to cover the area.

Making bows

Pretty bows make perfect decorations on Christmas cakes, whether used large or small.

1. Thinly roll the chosen colour on a surface dusted with cornflour (cornstarch). Cut out one long strip, then cut the strip into two rectangles. Dampen the ends then fold the rectangles over to form loops. Position on the cake, leaving a small gap between the loops and tucking rolls of absorbent kitchen paper inside the loops to hold them in shape.

2. Cut more long strips of the same thickness for bow ends. Finish the ends that will trail neatly with a knife. Pinch the other ends together and secure between the loops. Cut a square of icing, doming it slightly in the centre. Secure over the centre of the bow to hide all the ends. Remove the absorbent kitchen paper once hardened.

3. If liked, the bows can be further decorated by painting the edges with gold or silver, or painting random dots of colour.

Tip

● If doing a lot of decorative sugarpaste work, cut a 12cm (5 in) square of muslin and spoon a little cornflour (cornstarch) into the centre. Bring the edges over the cornflour and tie with an elastic band or string. 'Pat' the cornflour onto the surface when rolling the sugarpaste to give an even and economical dusting.

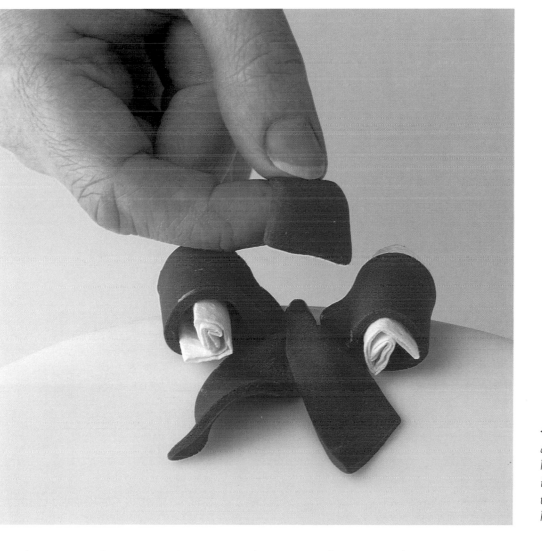

◀ *Tuck pieces of absorbent kitchen paper into the loops of the bow until hardened.*

QUICK-AND-EASY CAKES

Chocolate Box

Covered with star-embossed icing and finished with trailing ribbons and chocolate truffles, this effective cake combines simplicity with speed.

CAKE AND DECORATION

two 15cm (6 in) square rich or light fruit cakes
60ml (4 tbsp) apricot glaze · 1kg (2 lb) marzipan
(almond paste) · 1kg (2 lb) sugarpaste · icing
(confectioner's) sugar and cornflour (cornstarch)
for dusting · burgundy food colouring · 2m (2 yd)
green ribbon, 1-2cm (½-¾ in) wide (alternatively
use two or three contrasting ribbons) · 60g (2 oz)
icing (confectioner's) sugar · gold-coloured foil
about 500g (1 lb) selection of chocolate truffles
1m (1 yd) ribbon for board edge

EQUIPMENT

20cm (8 in) square gold cakeboard · small,
medium and large star cutters · paper piping bag

---

1 Trim any excessive domes from the surfaces of the cakes. Brush one cake top wth apricot glaze and invert the other cake onto it. Fill any gaps left around the edges with pieces of marzipan. Place the cake on the board and brush with the remaining apricot glaze.

TIP
The gold foil can be saved from bars of plain chocolate.

2 Roll out the marzipan and use to cover the cake, one side at a time. Colour the sugarpaste burgundy. Roll out a little and use to cover the top of the cake, trimming off excess around the edges. Roll out the remaining icing and use to cover the sides. If preferred, cover one side at a time and smooth out the joins using hands dusted with cornflour.

3 Dip the cutters in a little cornflour, then impress them gently into the sides of the cake, spacing the stars randomly and overlapping some.

4 Cut the ribbon into varying lengths between 20cm (8 in) and 30cm (12 in). Mix the icing sugar with a little water to make a fairly thin paste. Place in the piping bag and snip off the tip.

5 Use the icing in the bag to secure the ribbon lengths around the top edges of the cake, so that the loops or ends fall down the sides. Tear the foil into pieces and secure over the ribbon ends to resemble opened wrappings.

▲ *Secure the ribbon loops to the top edge of the cake, then stick foil over the ends.*

6 Arrange the chocolates over the top of the cake, piling them up in the centre. Secure the ribbon around the edge of the board.

Fruited 'Snow' Cake

A really easy 'fun' idea that mimics storybook Christmas cakes – laden with fruit and heavily topped with marzipan and peaking snow.

CAKE AND DECORATION

20cm (8 in) round rich or light fruit cake
45ml (3 tbsp) apricot glaze · 750 g (1½ lb) white
marzipan (almond paste) · 1kg (2 lb) sugarpaste
icing (confectioner's) sugar for dusting · brown
and yellow food colourings · 60g (2 oz) mixed
dried fruit · 15g (½ oz) glacé cherries, roughly
chopped · 15g (½ oz) blanched almonds, roughly
chopped · 500g (1 lb) yellow marzipan (almond
paste) · double quantity royal icing · sprig of holly
with berries · 1m (1 yd) ribbon for board edge

EQUIPMENT

25cm (10 in) round gold cakeboard · large
paintbrush · small piece of foam sponge
palette knife

TIP

If the holly has no berries, colour a little sugarpaste red and shape into small balls. Alternatively, make holly leaves from sugarpaste (see pages 11-12).

1 Brush the cake with apricot glaze and cover with the white marzipan. Place on the cakeboard. Cover with the sugarpaste.

2 Mix together a little brown and yellow food colouring and dilute with water. Brush over the sides of the cake with a large paintbrush to give a warm brown colour. (Test colour on a little paper or leftover icing first). Dot the sides of the cake with a darker brown colour, diluting it first with a little water if it is very thick. 'Stipple' the darker brown colour with the piece of foam so that the sugarpaste is smudged with colour like a fruit cake.

3 While the brown sugarpaste is still soft, press in small pieces of the dried fruit, almonds and cherries.

▲ *Embed pieces of dried fruit and nuts in the sugarpaste while it is still soft.*

4 Lightly knead the yellow marzipan then roll it out on a surface lightly dusted with icing sugar to a 25cm (10 in) round. Give it a very uneven edge so that it will create a wavy border around the top of the cake. Lightly dampen the top of the cake with water, then lay the marzipan in position, pressing down gently. The marzipan should come about halfway down the cake sides.

5 Spread the royal icing over the top of the cake and very slightly down the sides, using the palette knife. Swirl and peak the icing attractively as you work. Decorate the top of the cake with a sprig of holly and several berries. If you cannot find real holly, make it from sugarpaste. Secure the ribbon around the edge of the board.

Star Cake

For a quick-and-easy table centrepiece, try this sparkling cake, decorated with cut-out stars and plenty of glitzy ribbon.

CAKE AND DECORATION

18cm (7 in) round quantity rich or light fruit cake mixture · 60ml (4 tbsp) apricot glaze · 750g (1½ lb) marzipan (almond paste) · icing (confectioner's) sugar and cornflour (cornstarch) for dusting 1.5kg (3 lb) sugarpaste · violet and blue food colourings · 1m (1 yd) fine purple, silver or blue haberdashery cord · silver liquid colouring 1m (1 yd) wired blue ribbon · 1m (1 yd) wired silver ribbon · 1m (1 yd) blue or lilac ribbon for board edge

EQUIPMENT

25cm (10 in) star-shaped cake tin · 28cm (11 in) round or hexagonal silver cakeboard · crumpled foil · small, medium and large star cutters fine paintbrush

1 Line the star-shaped tin (see page 5). Turn the cake mixture into the tin and bake for the time stated in the quantities charts (see page 4 or 5). Leave to cool. Brush the cake with apricot glaze and cover with marzipan.

2 Colour 315g (10 oz) of the sugarpaste with a little violet food colouring. Lightly dampen the cakeboard. Thinly roll out the coloured paste and use to cover the cakeboard, trimming off excess around the edges. Leave to harden.

3 To make the stars, roll out 60g (2 oz) white sugarpaste. Lightly

press the crumpled foil over the icing to give a textured surface. Dip the cutters in a little cornflour, then cut out several stars in each size. Place on a sheet of greaseproof paper. Colour another 60g (2 oz) sugarpaste deep blue and another 60g (2 oz) a slightly darker shade of violet. Make more stars in these colours and leave to harden, preferably overnight.

4 Place the star cake on the board so that tips of the stars are in line with the points of a hexagonal board. Cover the cake with the remaining sugarpaste and trim off the excess around the base. Press the cord around the base of the star.

5 Use the silver colouring to paint the white stars. To arrange the ribbon, twist one of the wired ribbons around the fingers to coil it. Gently pull the ends apart. Twist the wires together at one end and press into the icing just above the cord around base of the star.

▲ *To create texture, press crumpled foil over sugarpaste before cutting out the stars.*

6 Tuck the other end of the ribbon into the cake on the other side, cutting off a little ribbon, if too long. Use the same technique for the other wired ribbon, laying it across the first.

7 Arrange the cut-out stars over the cake and around the board to decorate. Secure the ribbon around the edge of the board.

Mistletoe Garland

With its boldly contrasting colours and wreath of mistletoe, this cake is simply stunning.

CAKE AND DECORATION

20cm (8 in) round rich or light fruit cake
45ml (3 tbsp) apricot glaze · 1kg (2 lb) marzipan (almond paste) · 1.5kg (3 lb) sugarpaste · icing (confectioner's) sugar and cornflour (cornstarch) for dusting · dark blue, pale green, dark green and cream food colourings · gold dusting powder clear alcohol (gin or vodka) · 60g (2 oz) icing (confectioner's) sugar · 1m (1 yd) ribbon for board edge

EQUIPMENT

30cm (12 in) round silver cakeboard · greaseproof paper · dressmaker's pins · small piece of foam sponge · crumpled foil · fine paintbrush

1 Cover the cake with marzipan. Place on the cakeboard. Reserve 500g (1 lb) sugarpaste. Use the remainder to cover the cake and board.

2 Measure the circumference of the cake with a piece of fine string. Cut a strip of greaseproof paper the same length as the string and about 1cm (½ in) wide. Fold it in half and then in half twice more to make a strip of eight thicknesses. Unfold the paper and secure around the top edge of the sides with pins. Use a pin to mark around the top edge of the cake at each fold.

TIP
For a quicker version, use bought fabric rope and secure in position with a little icing.

3 Dilute a little blue food colouring. Dip in the piece of sponge, then use to lightly stipple the cake surface.

4 Colour 90g (3 oz) of the remaining sugarpaste pale green, another 90g (3 oz) dark green and a further 30g (1 oz) cream. Roll out the pale green icing and cut out small mistletoe leaves, about 4.5cm (1¾ in) long and 1cm (½ in) at the widest point. Mark veins down the centre and leave to harden on crumpled foil. Repeat with dark green to make 24 of each colour. Shape the cream icing into small balls for berries.

5 Thinly roll a little of the remaining sugarpaste to two long thin sausages, then twist them together to make a rope. Using a fine paintbrush, dampen the icing, just underneath the pin marks. Cut a 10cm (4 in) length of rope and secure around the side of the cake, with the ends meeting the pin marks. Repeat around the cake, securing a ball of icing at each point. Make long ropes and secure first around the base, then the board edge.

6 Mix a little gold dusting powder with clear alcohol. Using a fine paintbrush, paint dots on the cake and board. Carefully paint all the ropes.

7 Mix the icing sugar with water and place in a piping bag. Secure the leaves and berries. Secure the ribbon around the edge of the board.

▲ *Cut out the teardrop-shaped leaves.*

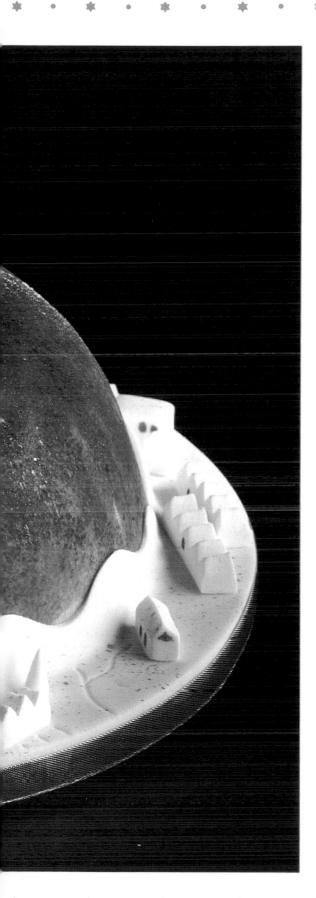

Santa Comes to Town

This magical scene of Father Christmas racing through the sky has great appeal to children. The sleigh and reindeer take a little time and patience, but a bought version can easily be substituted without decreasing the effect.

CAKE AND DECORATION

23cm (9 in) round rich or light fruit cake mixture
45ml (3 tbsp) apricot glaze · 750g (1½ lb) marzipan (almond paste) · icing (confectioner's) sugar and cornflour (cornstarch) for dusting
1.5kg (3 lb) sugarpaste · dark blue, orange and red food colourings · 1 quantity royal icing · silver dusting powder · clear alcohol (gin or vodka)
1m (1 yd) ribbon for board edge

EQUIPMENT

3.4 litre (6 pint) clear ovenproof bowl
33cm (13 in) round silver cakeboard · small piece of foam sponge · fine paintbrush · non-stick paper paper piping bag · fine writing tube (tip)

1 Grease the bowl and line the base with a circle of greaseproof paper. Turn the cake mixture into the bowl and level the surface. Bake for the time stated in the quantities chart (see page 4 or 5). Leave to cool, then remove from the bowl and level the

surface if excessively domed.

2 Invert the cake onto the board and brush with apricot glaze. Use a little marzipan to fill in any large gaps between the cake and board. Roll out the remaining marzipan to a 36cm (14 in) round and use to cover the cake, easing around the sides to fit. Trim off the excess. Use 1 kg (2 lb) of the sugarpaste to cover the cake in the same way, trimming off excess around the base.

3 Dilute a little blue food colouring with water. Dip the piece of sponge in the colouring, then use to lightly stipple the surface of the cake. (Practice on white paper or spare icing first).

4 Dampen the edges of the cakeboard. Roll out half the remaining sugarpaste to a long curved strip about 46cm (18 in) long and 5cm (2 in) wide. Cut a wavy line along the inner edge of the curve. Position the strip to half cover the cakeboard so that the wavy edge sits around the base of the cake. Cover the other half of the board in the same way, trimming off excess paste around the edge.

5 Use the remaining white sugarpaste to shape a selection of buildings such as houses, flats and a church. Position on the cakeboard. Paint some small lighted windows using the orange colouring.

6 Trace the sleigh and reindeer template (see page 78) onto a strip of non-stick paper. Beat some of the royal icing, adding a little water or lemon juice so that it just holds its shape. Place in a piping bag fitted with the writing tube. Lay another strip of non-stick paper over the template and pipe over the outline.

7 Once the outline is complete, fill in the body areas and sleigh with more icing. Make another runout in the same way then turn the template over and make two more runouts on separate pieces of paper. (This makes one set, plus a spare.)

8 Leave the icing runouts for about 48 hours to harden, then carefully peel away the paper. Mix a little silver dusting powder with clear alcohol until the consistency of thin paint. Use to decorate the runouts.

▶ *Position the strip of sugarpaste on the cakeboard, with the wavy edge against the cake.*

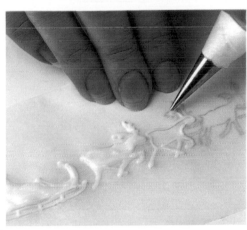

▲ *Lay non-stick paper over the sleigh and reindeer template and pipe over the design*

▲ *Simple shapes cut from sugarpaste make very effective buildings.*

◄ *Carefully secure the sleigh and reindeer runout to a sugarpaste block brushed with royal icing.*

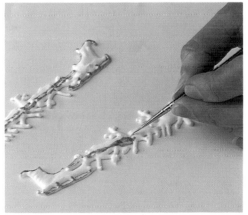

▲ *Once dry, decorate the runouts using silver dusting powder and clear alcohol mixed.*

9 Shape a small block of sugarpaste measuring 2 x 1 x 1cm (³⁄₄ x ¹⁄₂ x ¹⁄₂ in). Secure to the top of the cake, slightly off-centre. Brush the block with a little royal icing. Carefully secure the sleigh section of a runout to each side of the block.

10 Shape a small Father Christmas and tiny presents and position in the sleigh. Paint Father Christmas red. Using more silver colour, paint stars in various sizes onto the blue icing. Sprinkle more dusting powder around the sleigh by tapping the paintbrush against the back of the hand. Sprinkle more dusting powder over the buildings. Secure the ribbon around the edge of the board.

TIP
Handle the cake as little as possible once the icing runouts have been positioned. They are very fragile!

Carol Singers

The appeal of this cake is its strong Christmassy colours and simple details. The basic colours can easily be adjusted to suit personal taste.

CAKE AND DECORATION
23cm (9 in) round rich or light fruit cake
45ml (3 tbsp) apricot glaze · 1kg (2 lb) marzipan
(almond paste) · icing (confectioner's) sugar and
cornflour (cornstarch) for dusting · 2kg (4 lb)
sugarpaste · red, dark green, light green, yellow,
blue and black food colourings · icing
(confectioner's) sugar for sprinkling

EQUIPMENT
30cm (12 in) round silver cakeboard · medium
Christmas tree cutter · cocktail sticks (toothpicks)
fine paintbrush

1 Brush the cake with apricot glaze and cover with marzipan. Place on the cakeboard. Colour 1.25kg (2½ lb) of the sugarpaste red and use to cover the cake. Place a small bowl or saucer with a diameter of 12cm (5 in) on the centre of the cake. Cut around it and then lift out the red sugarpaste from the centre. Re-roll the red trimmings and use to cover the cakeboard. Reserve the trimmings.

2 Thickly roll 185g (6 oz) white icing and cut out a 12cm (5 in) round using the bowl or saucer. Lay the white icing in the centre of the cake, then smooth out gently with the palms of the hands. Reserve the white trimmings.

▲ *Cut out a 12cm (5 in) circle from white sugarpaste and place it in the centre of the cake.*

3 Taking the remaining icing, colour 185g (6 oz) dark green, 125g (4 oz) light green, 60g (2 oz) yellow, 60g (2 oz) blue, 30g (1 oz) pale pink (using a dash of red colouring, and colour the remainder black.

4 Thinly roll half the dark-green icing and cut out a 38 x 5cm (15 x 2 in) rectangle. Thinly roll half the pale-green icing and cut out several Christmas trees using the cutter. Lay the trees over the dark-green strip then gently roll with the rolling pin so that the trees are secured to the icing. Trim the edges of the strip. Lightly moisten one side of the cake and wrap the rectangle around it, pinching the ends together around the front to create a 'tie' in the scarf.

▼ *Bend lengths of green sugarpaste and score with a knife to resemble wool for the fringe.*

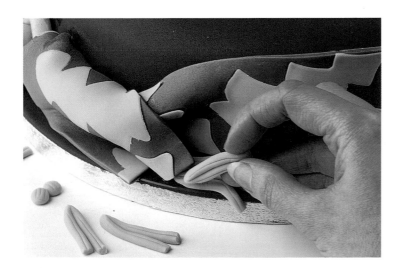

Shape and secure another rectangle around the other side of the cake. Shape two smaller scarf rectangles and secure to the front of the cake for the scarf ends.

5 Roll more pale-green icing under the palms of the hands to 7.5cm (3 in) lengths. Bend the lengths and make knife-marks to resemble threads of wool. Secure to one scarf end and finish with flattened balls of icing along the edge. Repeat on the other scarf end.

6 To make a character, shape a small pair of boots from black icing. Mould a rounded cone shape for the body and mark a line down the front. Position the body over the boots and secure together by pressing a cocktail stick right through to the base of the boots so that the figure stands upright. Add moulded arms, gloves and scarf. Roll a ball of icing and position for the head, adding a tiny ball of icing for the nose. Shape a hat and gently press into position.

▲ *Assemble the boots and body of each character first, then add the components.*

7 Shape the other figures in the same way, varying their clothes and colours. Position them on the cake. Dilute a little red and brown food colouring and use to paint the faces. Press the figures onto the cake then sprinkle lightly with icing sugar.

Father Christmas in Bed

This jolly cake provides a golden opportunity to play at modelling and painting. Older children can also have fun with the small decorative features.

CAKE AND DECORATION
20cm (8 in) square rich or light fruit cake
2kg (4 lb) sugarpaste · icing (confectioner's) sugar
and cornflour (cornstarch) for dusting · pale and
dark green, red, brown, yellow, blue and black
food colourings · 45ml (3 tbsp) apricot glaze
750g (1½ lb) marzipan (almond paste) · 1.2m (4 ft)
ribbon for board edge

EQUIPMENT
36cm (14 in) round silver cakeboard · small piece
of foam sponge · greaseproof paper · large
paintbrush · black icing pen

1 Cut off 4cm (1½ in) from one side of the cake to give the bed shape. Lightly dampen the cakeboard. Thinly roll 375g (12 oz) of the sugarpaste and use to cover the board. Trim off the excess icing around the edge of the board. Mix together a little of the pale-green and dark-green colourings and dilute with water. Dip

the piece of sponge in the colour then use to lightly stipple the surface of the cake. (Practice on a little white paper or spare white icing first.)

2 Brush the cake with apricot glaze. Reserve 185g (6 oz) of the marzipan. Roll out the remainder and use to cover the cake. Use half the remaining marzipan to shape a pillow, pressing it down in the centre. Roll the remainder into strips and lay over the bed to create folds. Position the cake on the cakeboard. Colour 500g (1 lb) of the sugarpaste pale green, 375g (12 oz) red, 60g (2 oz) pink, (using a dash of the red colouring) 60g (2 oz) black, 125g (4 oz) blue and 250g (8 oz) a soft brown, using a mixture of brown and yellow colourings. Leave the remainder white.

3 Trace the 'Father Christmas in bed' template on page 78 onto greaseproof paper and cut it out. Roll out the soft brown sugarpaste. Lay the template over the sugarpaste and cut around it. Carefully transfer to a piece of greaseproof paper. Mark the decorative edges with the tail-end of a paintbrush. Leave for 48 hours to harden.

▲ *Mark the decorative edging on the bedhead with the tail-end of a paintbrush.*

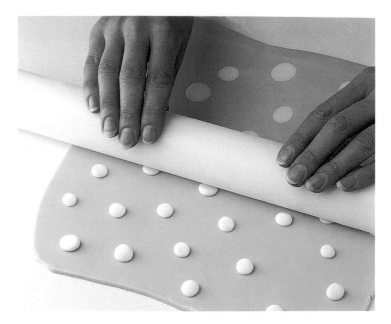

▲ *Gently press dots of white sugarpaste into the green, then roll lightly with a dusted rolling pin.*

5 Colour a little white sugarpaste dark green and cut out small holly leaves (see pages 11-12). Dampen the underside of the leaves and secure to the bedhead. Decorate with small ribbons of blue icing and tiny red berries. Secure small pieces of white icing to the marzipan at the top end of the bed. Lightly dampen, then press the bedhead gently into position.

6 Shape a ball of pink sugarpaste for the head. Add a small nose, then chubby cheeks and closed eyelids.

4 Roll out the pale-green sugarpaste to a 27cm (10½ in) square. Take small balls of white sugarpaste and press them lightly into the green. Dust a rolling pin with cornflour and roll it gently over the sugarpaste so that the white icing forms dots over the green. Carefully lift the icing over the cake, so that it just covers the pillow area at the head-end of the bed and falls down the sides of the cake.

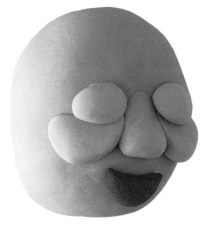

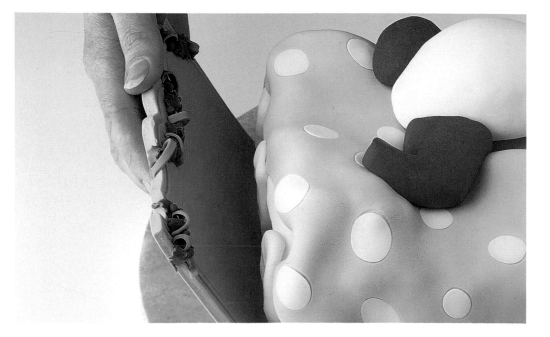

▶ *Dampen the sugarpaste at the top end of the bed, then press the bedhead into position.*

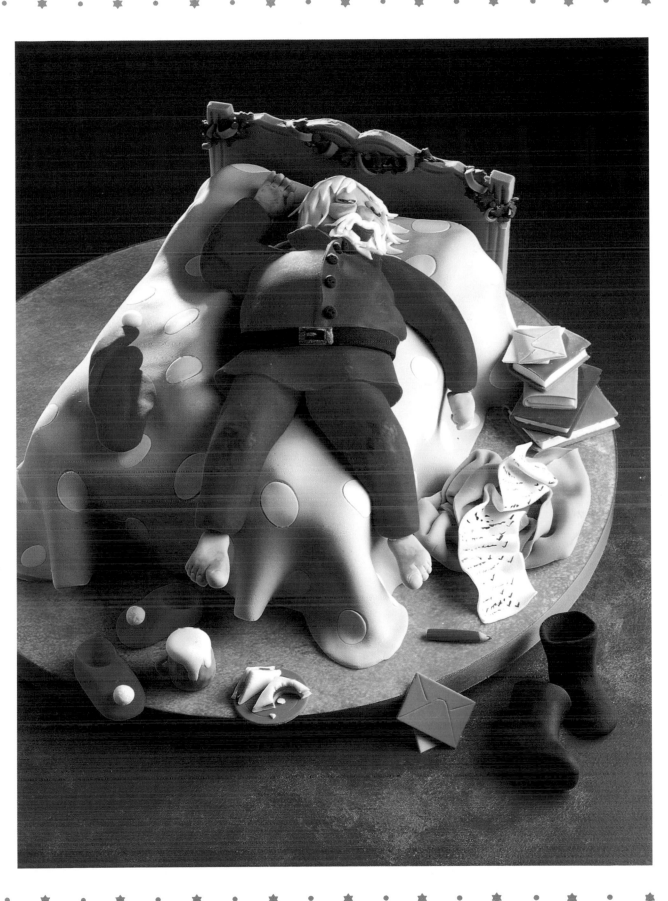

▶ *Make Father Christmas's hair from thin pieces of white paste applied in sections.*

Secure a small smiling mouth, made from red sugarpaste. Shape the remaining pink icing into hands and feet.

7 Position a large ball of white icing on the bed for Father Christmas's body. Shape and position chubby arms and legs from red sugarpaste. You will need about 60g (2 oz) for each leg and 30g (1 oz) for each arm. Position the head, hands and feet. Thinly roll more red icing and cut out a jacket, first positioning the strip below the waist and then two sections above, cutting and trimming to fit.

8 Roll and secure a black belt and buttons. From the remaining icing, shape a selection of items such as slippers, hat, Christmas cards, empty sack, glass of beer, snack, pencil and books. For the books, wrap coloured icing around rectangles of white.

9 For Father Christmas's hair, thinly roll a little white icing and cut into pieces. Lightly dampen the head then position the hair in sections. Finish with a small beard and moustache.

10 Position all the prepared accessories. Roll a long thin strip of white icing and lay loosely over the sack. Using the icing pen, write a ticked list on the icing and outline Father Christmas's eyes. Dilute a little red colouring and add a blush to his cheeks, hands and feet. Use a little diluted black colouring to make 'coal' marks on his knees and arms. Secure the ribbon around the edge of the board.

Christmas Nativity

The design of this cake is effective in its simplicity. Both the stable and figures are exceptionally easy to shape.

CAKE AND DECORATION

25cm (10 in) square rich or light fruit cake
60ml (4 tbsp) apricot glaze · 1.25kg (2½ lb)
marzipan (almond paste) · icing (confectioner's)
sugar and cornflour (cornstarch) for dusting
2.5kg (5 lb) sugarpaste · brown, purple, red, black,
dark- and light-blue, green and yellow food
colourings · 125g (4 oz) icing (confectioner's) sugar
1.5m (1½ yd) cream cord · 2m (2 yd) ribbon for
board edge

EQUIPMENT

30cm (12 in) square silver cakeboard · non-stick
paper · small star cutter · 4 and 5cm (1½ and
2 in) plain pastry cutters · cocktail stick
(toothpick) · paper piping bag · fine paintbrush

templates and two side templates). Roll and cut out a small star from white icing. Leave the star and stable to harden for 48 hours.

▲ *Cut around the stable template then carefully peel away the excess brown sugarpaste.*

2 Colour the remaining sugarpaste as follows: 90g (3 oz) purple, 90g (3 oz) red, 90g (3 oz) pale pink (using a dash of red colouring), 90g (3 oz) grey, (using a little black colouring), 60g (2 oz) dark blue, 60g (2 oz) pale blue and 30g (1 oz) green. Leave 30g (1 oz) white, then colour the remainder yellow.

3 Reserve 90g (3 oz) of the yellow icing. Roll the remainder to a thick sausage. Dot with 30g (1 oz) of the brown icing. Fold the ends of the icing into the centre and roll again so that the yellow icing becomes marbled with the

1 Brush the cake with apricot glaze and cover with marzipan. Place on the cakeboard. Colour 250g (8 oz) of the sugarpaste dark brown. Trace and cut out the stable templates on page 79 onto non-stick or greaseproof paper. Thinly roll the brown icing and lay on a sheet of non-stick paper. Lay the templates over the icing and cut around them, then carefully peel away the excess paste. (You will need two roof

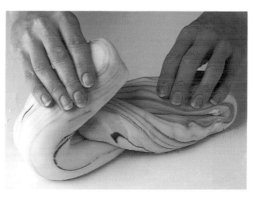

▲ *Dot a thick sausage of yellow sugarpaste with brown, fold and roll again to marble.*

brown. Continue rolling and folding until the colours are fairly evenly distributed. Roll out the icing and use to cover the cake and board. Trim off excess icing around the edges of the board.

4 To shape a 'king', make a small piece of purple-coloured icing into a cone shape. Shape two curved sections for the arms and secure to the cone. Shape head and hands from pink icing. For the cloak, cut a 5cm (2 in) circle of icing using the large cutter. Cut away an area for the neck, and position around the body. Shape a small circle of brown icing for the hair, then add the crown and gifts. Shape two more kings in the same way. Shape 'Mary' as above, draping a 4cm (1½ in) circle of dark blue icing over her head.

5 Shape the remaining characters in the same way, using a cocktail stick for the centre of the shepherd's crook. For Jesus in the manger, shape a simple base of brown icing. Roll a tiny ball of flesh-coloured icing for the head and lay it on a thinly rolled square of white icing. Wrap the white icing around the head and lay it on the base. For the

▼ *The simple figures consist of cone-shaped bodies with balls for heads and hands and circular cloaks.*

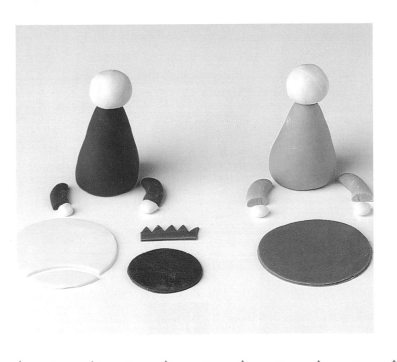

▲ *The donkey is made from nine pieces of grey sugarpaste and assembled into a sitting position.*

▶ *Pipe brown icing along the sides and roof of the stable to join the pieces together.*

7 Use a little more icing to pipe the donkey's mane. Secure the star to the stable roof. Using a little diluted brown colouring, paint simple features onto the faces then position the figures on the cake. Tie the cord around the cake and secure at the back with a little icing. Secure the ribbon around the edge of the board.

donkey, shape the grey icing as shown above and assemble so that the donkey is in a sitting position.

6 Mix the icing sugar with a little water to make a paste. Colour it dark brown and place in a piping bag. Snip off the tip. Pipe a little icing down one side of the stable back. Secure one side-piece to the back and position on the cake. Position the other side-piece and then the roof sections in the same way. Pipe another line of icing around the base of the stable.

Winter Wonderland

This beautiful cake, depicting a winter snow scene, takes a little more time to make than most, but the results are well worth the time and effort involved.

CAKE AND DECORATION

double quantity of 18cm (7 in) round rich or light fruit cake mixture · 60ml (4 tbsp) apricot glaze · 1kg (2 lb) marzipan (almond paste) · 1.5kg (3 lb) sugarpaste · icing (confectioner's) sugar and cornflour (cornstarch) for dusting · double quantity royal icing · blue and pearlized or white dusting powder · icing (confectioner's) sugar for sprinkling

EQUIPMENT

two 15cm (6 in) round cake tins · 33cm (13 in) petal or round silver cakeboard · non-stick paper paper piping bags · fine writing tube (tip) wooden cocktail sticks (toothpicks) · large soft paintbrush

1 Line the round cake tins (see page 5). Divide the cake mixture between the tins and bake for the time stated in the quantities chart (see page 4 or 5). Leave to cool. (If you only have one tin, bake one cake at a time.)

2 Level off the domes on top of the cakes if excessive. Brush the cakes with apricot glaze, then position one cake over the other, filling in the gaps left around the middle with marzipan. Place the cake on the board. Use three-quarters of the marzipan to cover the sides of the cake. Use the remainder to cover the top.

3 Roll out 1kg (2 lb) of the sugarpaste on a surface dusted with icing sugar to a 38cm (15 in) round. Lay over the top of the cake and ease around the sides. Cut off any excess bulk of icing around the sides, then smooth the icing with the palms of the hands to eliminate the creases. Trim off the excess around the base.

4 Position small mounds of the remaining sugarpaste on the board around the cake, varying them in height and diameter. Roll out half the remaining sugarpaste to a long curved strip. Trim the inner edge of the strip. Dampen the base of the cake around the mounds, then lay the strip in position so that the trimmed edge rests against the sides of the cake. Cover the other half of the board in the same way, smoothing out the joins and trimming off excess around the edge.

5 To make the trees, trace five of each tree template (see page 79) onto non-stick paper. Beat some of the royal icing, adding a little water or lemon juice so that it just holds its shape. Place in a piping bag fitted with the writing tube. Lay a large sheet of

▲ *Cover the cakeboard with sugarpaste, concealing the mounds beneath.*

▲ *Pipe icing into the tree outlines, easing it into the corners with a cocktail stick.*

TIP
If any of the trees will not readily stand unsupported, prop them up with a piece of absorbent kitchen paper until set.

non-stick paper over the large template and pipe over the outline. Move the templates under the paper and trace 35 more large trees. Use the same technique for the the other trees, making about 60 of the medium-size and 40 of the small.

6 Thin more of the royal icing with water until the surface is smooth and level when left to settle for several seconds. Place in a piping bag and snip off the merest tip. Pipe the icing into the tree outlines, easing the icing into the corners with a cocktail stick. Leave to set for about 48 hours.

7 Mix together a little blue and pearlized or white dusting powder. Using the large soft brush, gently dust the sides of the cake, making the colour slightly more dense near the base. (Practice on a little spare icing first to check that the blue is not too deep.)

8 Pipe small dots of icing over the top and sides of the cake to resemble snow, making the dots more dense near the base of the cake. Carefully peel the paper lining away from the icing trees. To assemble the trees, pipe a line of icing along the straight edge of a large tree shape. Gently secure the shape to the cake, letting the shaped edge stand slightly

away from the cake. Position another tree section against the cake so that the straight edges almost meet. Build up the tree with three more sections. Repeat at intervals around the cake using large and medium sections.

9 For the trees that stand away from the cake, pipe a dot of icing where the tree is to stand. Secure two tree sections together and position on the icing. Gradually build up the tree with more sections. (You will need six to seven for each tree). Continue adding trees to the cake, arranging some in clusters. Use a medium-size tree to decorate the top of the cake. Once set in position, dust the trees with a little sifted icing sugar.

▲ *Dust the sides of the cake with blue and white or pearlized dusting powder.*

▲ *To assemble the trees, pipe icing along the straight edge and press onto the cake.*

Partridge in a Pear Tree

This impressive cake should satisfy any demands for something different. The partridge takes time to mould and paint, but the rest is easy.

CAKE AND DECORATION

20cm (8 in) round quantity rich or light fruit cake mixture · 45ml (3 tbsp) apricot glaze · 750g (1½ lb) marzipan (almond paste) · icing (confectioner's) sugar and cornflour (cornstarch) for dusting · 2kg (4 lb) sugarpaste · burgundy, dark-green, yellow and light- and dark-brown food colourings · whole cloves · gold liquid colouring dark green dusting powder · 1.5m (5 ft) ribbon for board edge

EQUIPMENT

2.3 litre (4 pint) clear ovenproof bowl 40cm (16 in) round silver cakeboard · cocktail sticks (toothpicks) · piping tube (tip) · fine paintbrush · large leaf cutter · leaf veiner crumpled foil

1 Grease the bowl and line the base with a circle of greaseproof paper. Turn the cake mixture into the bowl and level the surface. Bake for the time stated in the quantities chart (see page 4 or 5). Leave to cool, then remove from the bowl and level the surface if the top is excessively domed.

2 Invert the cake onto the cakeboard and fill any gaps left between

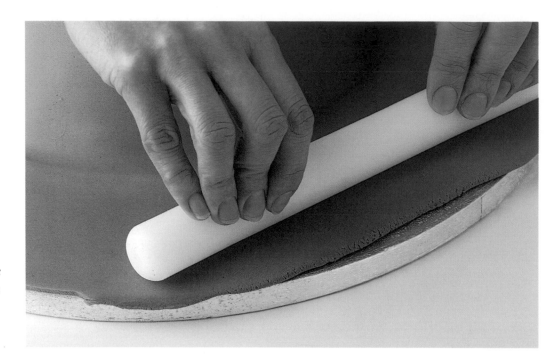

▶ *If necessary, use a small rolling pin to ease the paste out to the edge of the board.*

the cake and the board with marzipan. Brush the cake with apricot glaze and cover with the remaining marzipan. Reserve 375g (12 oz) of the sugarpaste. Colour 125g (4 oz) burgundy, then colour the remainder dark green. Reserve 250g (8 oz) of the dark-green sugarpaste.

3 Roll out the remaining dark-green sugarpaste to a large round, about 43cm (17 in) in diameter. Carefully lift the icing over the cake. Using the palms of the hands, smooth the icing down the sides and over the board until completely covered. If necessary, roll a small rolling pin from the base of the cake out to the edge of the board so that it is completely covered. Trim off the excess paste around the edge and reserve.

4 To make the partridge, roll 125g (4 oz) of the white sugarpaste into a smooth ball. Gently mould and stretch the paste, forming a small head at one end and a peaked tail at the other. Using a cocktail stick, impress a wing

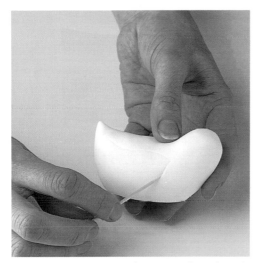

▲ *Impress a wing outline onto the sides of the partridge with a cocktail stick.*

outline onto either side of the bird. Mark a simple feather outline by impressing the thick end of a piping tube into the sides.

5 Colour a tiny ball of icing yellow and shape a small beak. Secure to the head. Mark the position of the eyes with the cocktail stick. Use a little diluted dark-brown colouring to paint the areas around the eyes and neck. Mix the two brown colourings to make a lighter shade and use to paint the back of the partridge, bringing the colour to a point at the top of the beak.

6 Make a very diluted, pale-brown colour by adding a little yellow and use it to paint the wing areas, adding strokes of darker brown to accentuate the feathers. Leave the bird to harden on a piece of greaseproof paper.

7 To make the leaves, very thinly roll a little dark-green sugarpaste and cut out leaf shapes. Roll the edges with a cocktail stick to lightly curl. Press onto a leaf veiner, then transfer to a piece of crumpled foil to harden. (Make a few at a time so that the icing does not dry out. You will need about 70 leaves altogether). Leave to harden for 24 hours.

8 To make the pears, lightly knead the remaining 250g (8 oz) white sugarpaste and divide into seven pieces. Make each into a pear shape. Remove

▼ *Paint the partridge's back, bringing the colour to a point above the beak.*

▲ *Cut out leaf shapes, press onto a veiner, then curl the edges. Leave to harden on crumpled foil.*

ball to secure in a propped-up position. Continue adding leaves, overlapping them slightly and varying the angles and direction. As you get towards the top of the cake, position the partridge, propping it up with more green icing, so that the beak is pointing upwards. The leaves around the bird should then hide the base. To secure the pears at intervals, press cocktail sticks into the cake so that only 2cm (¾ in) is exposed. Push a pear gently onto each cocktail stick.

the round ends of the cloves, then press a clove into the base of each pear. Press cloves into the other ends to resemble stalks. Paint the pears gold.

9 Start near the base of the cake when securing the leaves. Take pea-sized balls of green icing trimmings and press onto the cake. Lightly dampen the surface then gently press a leaf onto the

10 Thinly roll the burgundy icing and cut out some 12 x 1cm (5 x ½ in) strips. Lightly twist the strips and lay around the edges of the board with the ends meeting, slightly away from the edge. Shape simple bows (see page 13) and position where the strips meet. Shape several more bows and assemble them among the leaves.

11 Paint small dots of gold colour onto all the ribbons. Secure the ribbon around the edge of the board.

▶ *Press cocktail sticks into the cake at intervals, then push each pear onto a stick.*

Floating Candles

Elaborately finished with pretty candles and trailing ivy leaves, this stunning cake doubles up as a dinner-table centrepiece for festive party gatherings.

CAKE AND DECORATION

18cm (7 in) round quantity rich or light fruit cake mixture · 1kg (2 lb) sugarpaste · dark-green and pink food colourings · icing (confectioner's) sugar and cornflour (cornstarch) for dusting · 45ml (3 tbsp) apricot glaze · 1kg (2 lb) marzipan (almond paste) · 7 small round 'floating' candles 1 quantity royal icing · 30g (1 oz) bought petal paste · pink lustre dusting powder · piping jelly 1m (1 yd) ribbon for board edge · decorative glass beads

EQUIPMENT

2.3 litre (4 pint) clear ovenproof bowl · 5cm (2 in) round cutter · 30cm (12 in) round silver cakeboard · small and large ivy cutters · leaf veiner · green floristry wire · crumpled foil · fine paintbrush · large soft paintbrush · green floristry tape

TIP
If wax runs onto the cake surface this can easily be removed with the piping jelly before serving.

1 Grease the ovenproof bowl and line the base with a circle of greaseproof paper. Turn the cake mixture into the bowl and level the surface. Bake for the time stated in the quantities chart (see page 4 or 5). Leave to cool, then remove from the bowl and level the surface if excessively domed.

2 Using the cutter as a guide, mark out seven circles, at irregular intervals, on the surface of the cake. Take a teaspoon and scoop out a little of the cake within the marked areas to allow room for the candles to sit.

▲ *Scoop out pieces of cake with a teaspoon to seat the candles.*

3 Colour 315g (10 oz) of the sugarpaste dark green. Lightly dampen the cakeboard. Thinly roll the green icing and use to cover the board. Trim off excess icing around the edge of the board.

4 Brush the top of the cake with a little apricot glaze. Roll out a generous third of the marzipan and use to cover the top of the cake, pressing the paste into the hollowed-out sections. Invert the cake onto a piece of greaseproof paper or foil and brush with the remaining glaze. Cover the base and sides with the remaining marzipan.

5 Colour the remaining sugarpaste pink and reserve 185g (6 oz). Roll out the remainder and use to cover the base and sides of the cake. Turn the cake the right way up and position on the iced board. Roll out the remaining pink icing under the palms of the hands to make a long thin rope. Dampen the rim of the cake and lift the rope into

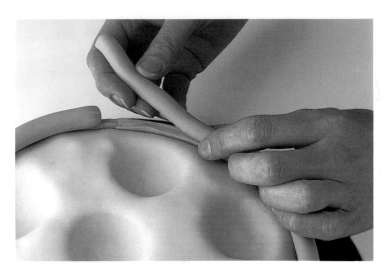

▲ *Dampen the rim of the cake and press the pink rope into position. Trim the ends to fit.*

▼ *Press the ivy leaves onto a veiner then add the wires. When dry, dust the leaves green.*

position. Trim the ends to fit, then smooth out the join.

6 Position the candles on the surface of the cake. Colour the royal icing a paler shade of pink and thin it with a little lemon juice or water until the surface becomes level when left to stand for several seconds. Spoon the icing around the candles. Leave to set overnight.

7 To make the ivy leaves, take a small ball of petal paste, about the size of a large pea. Use the handle of the paintbrush to roll the paste as thinly as possible, leaving a thicker area in the centre for wiring. Press out the ivy

shape with a cutter, then press the leaf gently onto the leaf veiner. Cut a 7.5cm (3 in) length of floristry wire and bend over the tip to shape a hook. Press into the base of the ivy leaf. Bend the leaf slightly to create a realistic shape then place on a piece of foil to harden. Make more leaves in the same way – about 20 large and 25 small. To finish the leaves, dot the centres with a little green dusting powder, then brush the powder outwards with a fine brush.

8 Using a large soft paintbrush, coat the icing rim with pink dusting powder. Beat the piping jelly until smooth then brush it thickly over the royal icing around the candles.

9 Twist two or three small ivy leaves together into a bunch, then twist in one or two larger leaves, securing all the ends together with floristry wire. Arrange the leaves around the candles, bending some of the wires so that the leaves fall over the sides of the bowl. (Because the leaves are fragile, it is sometimes easier to bend the wires with tweezers.)

10 Secure the ribbon around the edge of the board. Scatter the glass beads around the cake to decorate.

▲ *Twist the wires of several leaves. Trail around the candles and over the sides.*

Christmas Storybooks

Christmas story characters, like Father Christmas's elves and chubby snowmen, all come together on this jolly cake. This is a cake for enthusiasts, as shaping both the books and the characters takes a little time.

CAKE AND DECORATION

25cm (10 in) square rich or light fruit cake
90ml (6 tbsp) apricot glaze · 1.5kg (3 lb) marzipan (almond paste) · icing (confectioner's) sugar and cornflour (cornstarch) for dusting · 2.5kg (5 lb) sugarpaste · yellow, black, orange, red, green, brown and black food colourings · 1 quantity royal icing · gold dusting powder · clear alcohol (gin or vodka) · small piece of rice paper · white edible glitter · 1.5m (1½ yd) ribbon for board edge

EQUIPMENT

30cm (12 in) square silver cakeboard · 12cm (5 in) square silver cake card · large writing tube (tip) paper piping bag · fine paintbrush

1 Cut any dome off the top of the cake so that it is completely flat. Using a large serrated knife, carefully cut the cake in half horizontally using a sawing action to make two thin slabs of cake. Cut a 2.5cm (1 in) slice off one side of one slab. (The large rectangle forms the largest book). Cut a third off

▲ *Using a serrated knife, cut the cake into rectangles.*

the other slab and halve this widthways. (This will form the opened book.) Halve the remaining rectangle of this slab to shape the middle two books.

2 Trim the edges of one long side from the three largest cakes to shape the spine. Place the largest cake on the board at an angle, and brush

with apricot glaze. Thinly roll some marzipan. Cut strips to cover the straight sides of the cake, then cover the top and spine side with another piece.

3 Colour the sugarpaste as follows: 500g (1 lb) yellow, 375g (12 oz) black, 375g (12 oz) orange, 375g (12 oz) red, 60g (2 oz) green and 60g (2 oz) pale pink (using a little red food colouring). Leave the remaining 750g (1½ lb) white. Use about half the red icing to cover the cakeboard, trimming off the excess around the edge.

4 Thinly roll a little white icing and use to cover three sides of the cake. Using the blade of a long knife, gently impress the 'pages.' Thinly roll a long strip of yellow icing and cut out a long thin strip. Secure a strip around the base of the white-iced sides, mitring the corners to neaten.

5 Roll out more yellow icing to a rectangle measuring the width of the book, including the spine, and the depth. Carefully lay the icing over the cake so that it only just comes over the

TIP

If preferred, paint some simplified sheet music onto the open book, or paint a simple Christmas poem or rhyme. This is best done with an icing pen once the sugarpaste has hardened.

▲ *Secure a strip of yellow sugarpaste around the base, mitring the corners neatly.*

◄ *Carefully lay another piece of yellow sugarpaste over the top, to form the cover.*

white sides, and fits around the spine. If the icing has stretched a little while lifting, ease it to fit and if necessary, trim off the excess.

6 Position another cake over the first, changing the angle. Glaze, cover with marzipan and white icing as before, then use black icing for the cover. Assemble the third cake, using orange icing for the cover. For the open book, lay the shaped cake on the cake card and cover with marzipan. Thinly roll more white icing and lay over the cake, easing around the sides to fit.

7 Press the icing into the centre, then gently press with the back of a knife to give a deep groove. Impress more page markings with a knife. Place the opened book cake in position and finish the edges with a band of black icing. Using diluted food colouring, paint decorative designs onto the pages of the open book.

8 Place the icing in the piping bag fitted with the writing tube. Use to pipe the decorative borders on the covers. Leave the piped icing to harden for several hours. Mix a little dusting powder with clear alcohol until the consistency of thin paint. Use to paint the borders.

9 To make an elf, mould red, green, pink and brown sugarpaste into the shapes shown in the photograph,

▼ *For the open book, cover the shaped cake with white sugarpaste, easing it over the sides.*

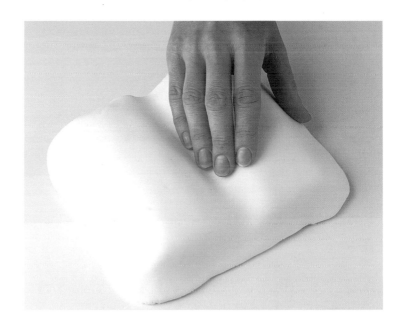

▲ *Pinch the sugarpaste to make the hat fall over the elf's face.*

remainder to mould and cut a body. Secure to the cake, bending one leg up on a book, and the other on the board. Add a small crumpled hat, buttons, eyes, mouth and carrot nose.

11 Shape several more Christmas characters using the remaining sugarpaste. For Father Christmas, build him up, starting with the boots, then adding trousers, tunic, head, arms and hat. Use the icing in the piping bag to pipe wiggly lines of hair, moustache, cuffs and bobble on the hat.

12 Shape a simple angel using a cone-shaped base. Add more piped icing for the angel's curly hair. For the wings, trace and cut out the template on page 78, and secure to the back of the body. Paint the piped icing with gold colouring.

13 Shape and secure more Christmas characters such as Scrooge, choirboys or carol singers. Dilute a little brown food colouring with water and use to paint features on the characters. Scatter the cake with the edible glitter. Secure ribbon around the edge of the board.

assembling them on the cake as they are moulded, stretching and bending the limbs. Arrange the hat so that it falls down over the elf's face.

10 To shape a snowman, take 60g (2 oz) white sugarpaste. From this mould a small head. Use the

▶ *First, roll a ball for the snowman's head, then mould and cut the body shape as shown.*

SMART AND TRADITIONAL

Holly Garland Cake

Simple decorations such as holly leaves, candy canes, baubles and presents are cleverly combined on this cake for traditionalists who are looking for something a little different.

CAKE AND DECORATION

25cm (10 in) round quantity rich or light fruit cake mixture, baked in a 25cm (10 in) petal-shaped tin · 60ml (4 tbsp) apricot glaze · 1.25kg (2½ lb) marzipan (almond paste) · icing (confectioner's) sugar and cornflour (cornstarch) for dusting · 2kg (4 lb) sugarpaste · red, dark-green and blue food colourings · silver dusting powder · 90g (3 oz) icing (confectioner's) sugar 1m (1 yd) fine cord

EQUIPMENT

33cm (12 in) petal-shaped silver cakeboard · large and small holly cutters · crumpled foil · fine paintbrush · paper piping bag

1 Brush the cake with apricot glaze and cover with marzipan, pressing it into the flutes of the petal shape. Trim off the excess. Cover the cake with 1.3kg (2¾ lb) of the sugarpaste.

2 From the remaining sugarpaste colour 185g (6 oz) red, 250g (8 oz) green and 60g (2 oz) blue, leaving the remainder white. Use the red icing to cover the cakeboard, trimming off the excess around the board edge. Reserve the trimmings.

3 Thinly roll a little green icing and cut out eight large holly leaves. Mark the central veins with a knife, then lay them over the crumpled foil to set in curved positions. To make the candy canes, very thinly roll a little white sugarpaste under the palms of the hands. Thinly roll a little red paste to the same thickness. Twist the rolls together, then roll them together. Cut into 3cm (1¼ in) lengths and bend over the tops. You will need about 12 altogether. Make four or five thicker, longer canes in the same way for the top of the cake.

4 From the blue icing shape 12 small squares, about 5mm (¼ in) in diameter and four larger squares, about 2cm (¾ in) in diameter. Very thinly roll red icing trimmings and use to shape ribbons for the larger parcels. From the remaining white icing roll 48 tiny balls of icing and 10 larger balls, about 1cm (½ in) in diameter. Leave all the decorations to harden for 24 hours.

5 Roll out some green icing under the palms of the hands to a sausage, a scant 1cm (½ in) thick. Cut a

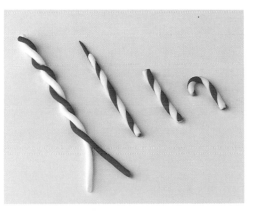

▲ *To make the candy canes, roll strips of white and red paste together.*

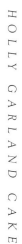

section of the icing and secure around one petal of the cake, so that the end comes 1cm (½ in) from the top edge of the cake and lowest part comes about 2cm (¾ in) from the base. Secure with a dampened paintbrush. Repeat around all sections of the cake.

6 Thinly roll more green icing and cut out holly leaves using the small cutter. Mark the central veins with a knife. Dampen the underside of the leaves then secure them to the green ropes around the sides of the cake to make a garland.

7 Lightly brush the small and large baubles with silver dusting powder. Mix the icing sugar with a little water to make a fairly thin paste. Place in the paper piping bag and snip off the tip. Use to secure the small baubles, candy canes and parcels to the garlands around the sides.

8 Use the larger decorations to make an attractive arrangement on the top of the cake, first securing the leaves and parcels, propping them up on small balls of foil until set in position. Then arrange the candy canes and baubles. Arrange the cord around the base of the cake, securing with a little icing.

▼ *Dampen the backs of the holly leaves and secure, at an angle, across the green ropes.*

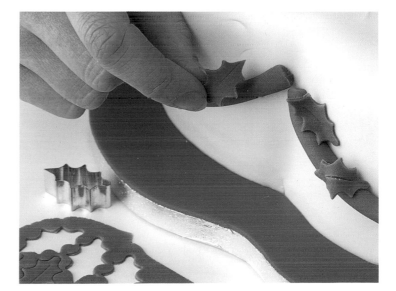

Jewelled Boxes

These pretty cakes, resembling little trinket boxes, make lovely presents for those who would have no need for a large cake. Choose your own colour scheme to suit the recipient – rich and bold or delicate and pretty.

CAKE AND DECORATION

18cm (7 in) round quantity rich or light fruit cake mixture · 60ml (4 tbsp) apricot glaze · 1kg (2 lb) marzipan (almond paste) · 1.5kg (3 lb) sugarpaste icing (confectioner's) sugar and cornflour (cornstarch) for dusting · red, blue and green food colourings · piping jelly · 1 quantity royal icing gold dusting powder · clear alcohol (gin or vodka)

EQUIPMENT

six empty, clean 440g (14 oz) food cans with both ends removed · six 10cm (4 in) round gold cake cards · paper piping bag · medium writing tube (tip) · fine paintbrush

1 Place the food cans on a baking sheet and line with greaseproof paper as you would a round cake tin (see page 5). Divide the cake mixture among the cans and bake for about 1 hour or until a skewer, inserted into the centres, comes out clean. Leave to cool in the tins.

2 Brush the cakes with apricot glaze. Roll out 250g (8 oz) of the marzipan and use to cover the tops of the cakes. Roll out the remaining marzipan and cut out six rectangles, each the circumference and depth of the cakes. Use to cover the sides of the cakes as shown below, then position them on the cake cards.

▲ *Cover the tops, then roll the cakes onto rectangles of marzipan to cover the sides.*

3 Divide 1kg (2 lb) of the sugarpaste into six portions. Use a portion to cover each cake, trimming off excess icing around the bases. From the remaining sugarpaste, colour 250g (8 oz) red, 125g (4 oz) blue and 125g (4 oz) green. Take pea-sized balls of the colours, and shape into small teardrop shapes. Use to decorate the top and sides of the cake, pressing down gently and leaving small gaps between the decorations. Leave the top centre area of each cake clear to allow for the ribbons.

4 Place the royal icing in a piping bag fitted with the writing tube. Use to pipe a border of icing around each coloured shape. Leave for several hours or overnight to harden.

5 Mix a little gold dusting powder with clear alcohol until the consistency of thin paint. Using a fine paintbrush, carefully paint over the piped icing. Lightly beat the piping jelly,

TIP

There are many other simple ways to prettily decorate small cakes. The white icing can be impressed with small festive cutters and then painted. Alternatively, decorate the cakes with coloured cut-out shapes.

▶ *Pull off pea-sized pieces of coloured paste and shape into teardrops. Arrange on cakes.*

then paint it over the coloured icing to give a glazed appearance.

6 To make a bow, thinly roll some red icing and cut out long strips about 3cm (1¼ in) wide. Use to assemble the bows on the tops of the cakes (see page 13). Prop up the bows with small pieces of absorbent kitchen paper until they harden. To add a touch of glamour, paint thin lines of gold along the edges of the ribbons to finish.

◀ *Pipe a border around each teardrop with a medium writing tube.*

Marzipan Fruits Cake

Heavily laden with realistic-looking moulded fruits, and boldly decorated with richly coloured ribbons and baubles, this cake makes a wonderful party centrepiece.

CAKE AND DECORATION

18cm (7 in) round rich or light fruit cake · 45ml (3 tbsp) apricot glaze · 1.75kg (3½ lb) marzipan (almond paste) · icing (confectioner's) sugar and cornflour (cornstarch) for dusting · 750g (1½ lb) sugarpaste · cream, green, red, burgundy, black and orange food colourings · whole cloves · gold, bronze and green dusting powder · clear alcohol (gin or vodka) · 2m (2 yd) wired gold ribbon, about 2.5cm (1 in) wide · 3m (3 yd) dusty blue or pink paper ribbon · 0.7m (27 in) fine cord

EQUIPMENT

25cm (10 in) round gold cakeboard · crumpled foil fine paintbrush · fine grater · floristry wire

1 Brush the cake with apricot glaze and cover with 750g (1½ lb) of the marzipan. Place on the board. Colour 500g (1 lb) of the sugarpaste cream and use to cover the cake. Leave to harden overnight.

2 For the cape gooseberries, thinly roll a little white sugarpaste and cut out a leaf shape, about 5cm (2 in) long and 2cm (¾ in) at the widest point. Press between two thicknesses of crumpled foil to texture it. Line several sections of a tartlet tin with crumpled foil and lay the leaf inside a foil section. Make three more leaves to complete one gooseberry, then make two more.

3 From the remaining sugarpaste roll 30 small balls about 2cm (¾ in) diameter. Leave to harden with the leaves for 24 hours.

4 To make the figs, roll 500g (1 lb) of the marzipan into seven balls. Pull a piece up into a point, keeping the paste as smooth as possible. Cut off the tip of the point. Colour the tip and about a third of the way down each fig with diluted green food colouring. Dilute a little burgundy colouring and smudge over the rest of the fig with the fingertips to give a base colour. Mix together some undiluted red and burgundy colouring and use to

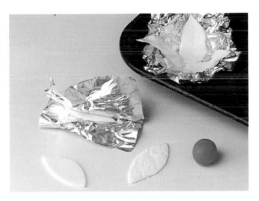

▲ *For the cape gooseberries, cut out leaves and press with crumpled foil to add texture.*

▲ *To make the figs, roll some balls, give each a point, then cut off the tips before colouring.*

TIP

Paper ribbon is more difficult to work with than the wired. If preferred use wired ribbon, in an equally bold colour, instead.

▼ *Thread the baubles onto each length of wire. Press the ends into the cake for a necklace effect.*

paint lines down the figs. (Add a little black colouring if colours are too bright.) Smudge the lines lightly to blend in.

5 For the clementines, divide another 185g (6 oz) marzipan into three. Shape each into a ball and flatten slightly. Roll over a fine grater to texture slightly. Remove the round ends from the cloves, then press a clove into each clementine. Paint with orange colouring. Use another 125g (4 oz) of the marzipan to shape small kumquats, each about 3cm (1¼ in) long. Texture and paint as for the clementines. Colour another 30g (1 oz) orange and use to shape little balls for the centres of the cape gooseberries. Colour the remainder pale green and roll into small balls for grapes.

6 Cut six 20cm (8 in) lengths of floristry wire and thread five baubles onto the centre of each. Take one piece and press the ends into the icing around the top edge of the cake, then let the baubles fall like a necklace down the sides. Arrange the remaining five pieces in the same way.

7 Cut six 25cm (10 in) lengths of wired ribbon and six 25cm (10 in) lengths of the paper ribbon. Fold each

in half and twist a little floristry wire around the centre. Fold back the ends and trim the twisted wire to a 2cm (¾ in) length. Loop the remaining paper ribbon around the cake so that it creates a garland below the beading. Secure around the top edge of the cake with more wire. Press a gold and coloured ribbon decoration into the icing at the top of each garland.

8 Secure the cord around the base of the cake. Mix the icing sugar with a little water to make a thick paste. Gradually pile the fruits onto the top of the cake, starting with a couple of figs and clementines on the base. Gradually build up the decoration to look like a fruit bowl, assembling the grapes to resemble a bunch. To assemble the cape gooseberries, place a dot of the prepared icing at the point where you want the base of the fruit to be. Secure the ends of four leaves in the icing, then push an orange centre onto each.

9 Mix a little gold dusting powder with clear alcohol and use to paint the cape gooseberry leaves. Mix the bronze dusting powder with more alcohol and use to paint the baubles. Lightly dust the grapes with a little green dusting powder to finish.

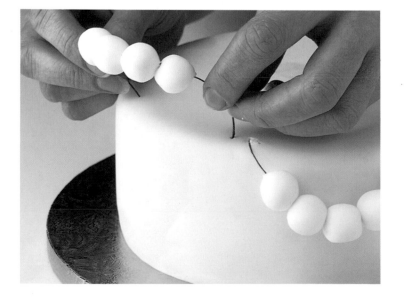

▲ *Loop the paper ribbon around the cake to create a garland below the beading.*

Candle Ring

Complete with realistic-looking 'dripping wax' and 'wrought-iron' candle holder, this impressive ring cake makes an artistic Christmas decoration.

CAKE AND DECORATION
18cm (7 in) round quantity rich or light fruit cake mixture · 45ml (3 tbsp) apricot glaze · 750g (1½ lb) marzipan (almond paste) · icing (confectioner's) sugar and cornflour (cornstarch) for dusting · 2kg (4 lb) sugarpaste · dark green, black, cream, yellow and orange food colourings 5 mini rolls · 1m (1 yd) ribbon for board edge sprigs of holly

EQUIPMENT
1.7 litre (3 pint) ring tin · 30cm (12 in) round silver cakeboard · 5 x 7cm (3 in) round silver cake cards · cocktail sticks (toothpicks) · fine paintbrush

1 Line the ring tin (see page 5). Turn the cake mixture into the tin and bake for the time stated in the quantities chart (see page 4 or 5). Leave to cool. Turn the cake out of the tin and round off the dome if excessive so that the cake sits comfortably when inverted.

2 Place the cake on the board and brush with apricot glaze. Roll out the marzipan to a 36cm (14 in) round. Lay it over the cake and ease the marzipan around the sides. Trim off the excess. Carefully press the marzipan in the centre of the cake down into the

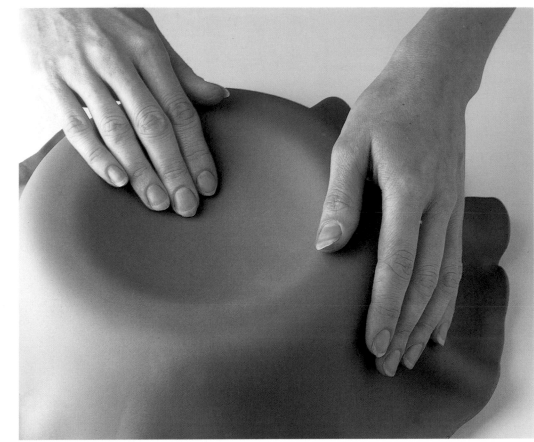

▶ *Ease the green paste over the cake, smoothing out the creases and pressing it into the cavity.*

TIP

For an impressive shortcut-version of this cake, use sturdy, real candles instead of the icing ones, but never leave lighted candles unattended. If using icing candles, some can be made shorter than others for a more realistic appearance.

cavity to create a pronounced dip.

3 Colour 1kg (2 lb) of the sugarpaste green, 375g (12 oz) black and the remainder cream. Roll out the green icing to a 36cm (14 in) round. Lift it over the cake, easing the icing around the sides and over the cakeboard, smoothing out creases and carefully pressing the icing into the centre of the cake. Trim off the excess paste around the edge of the board.

4 Roll out 125g (4 oz) of the black sugarpaste under the palms of the hands to create a long rope. Lightly dampen the upper part of the cake ring, then position the black icing in a ring around the top of the cake. Flatten the rope slightly with the fingertips.

5 Roll out more black icing to a rope 12cm (5 in) long. Roll up one end slightly, then position against one side of the cake so that the rolled end sits on

the board and other end meets the icing on top of the cake. Make and position four more in the same way, spacing them evenly around the sides of the cake.

6 Thinly roll out the remaining black sugarpaste. Lightly dampen the cake cards and cover with the icing. Position on the cake over the joins in the black icing.

7 To make the candles, roll out a little cream sugarpaste to a rectangle the circumference of a mini roll and 2.5cm (1 in) longer. Wrap around a mini roll to completely cover, smoothing out the join with the fingertips, and pinching the ends together. For the 'lighted' end of the candle, mould the excess icing to resemble melted wax. Carefully stand the candle on the other end, trimming off the excess icing if necessary, so that it stands upright.

8 Secure the candle to the cake. Shape and position four more in the same way. For the flames, roll small balls of cream icing and pull a little icing into a point. Push onto cocktail sticks and then press into the candle tops so that a little of the stick is still visible. For the dripping wax, mould long teardrop shapes from icing trimmings and secure to the sides of the candles. Use more icing to shape melted wax around the black candle bases.

9 Using a fine paintbrush, paint the flames with diluted yellow and orange colourings. Secure the ribbon around the edge of the board. Decorate the cake with sprigs of holly.

▶ *Position the black ropes vertically on the cake side, with the curled ends on the board.*

▼ *To make the candles, cover mini-rolls with cream-coloured sugarpaste.*

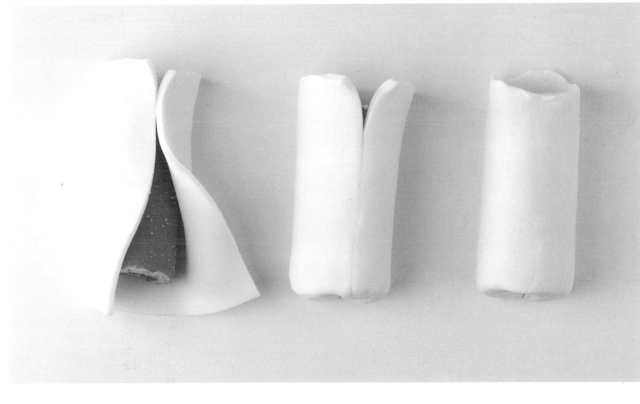

Glacé Christmas Ring

Not everyone likes the sweetness of icing. This beautiful Christmas ring cake is covered with marzipan (almond paste) and lavishly decorated with stunning glacé fruits.

CAKE AND DECORATION

18cm (7 in) round quantity rich or light fruit cake mixture · 90ml (6 tbsp) apricot glaze · 1kg (2 lb) marzipan (almond paste) · icing (confectioner's) sugar for dusting · three 30cm (12 in) lengths of fine gold ribbon · 9 cinnamon sticks approximately 750g (1½ lb) mixed glacé fruits such as cherries, strawberries, pineapple, orange slices, pears, figs and apricots · several whole star anise

EQUIPMENT

1.7 litre (3 pint) ring tin · 28cm (11 in) round gold cakeboard

TIP
Glacé fruits have a long shelf life, so even after decorating this cake can be stored, loosely covered, for weeks.

1 Line the ring tin (see page 5). Turn the cake mixture into the tin and bake for the time stated in the quantities chart (see page 4 or 5). Leave to cool. Turn the cake out of the tin and cut off the dome if excessive so that the cake sits comfortably when inverted. Position the cake on the board and brush with half of the apricot glaze.

2 Roll out the marzipan to a 30cm (12 in) round. Lay it over the cake, pressing well into the dip in the centre, and easing to fit around the sides. Trim off the excess around the sides, then cut out the piece of marzipan that falls inside the ring. Re-roll with the trimmings and use to line the centre of the cake.

3 Using a little of the fine gold ribbon, tie the cinnamon sticks into bundles of three.

4 Cut any large pieces of the glacé fruits into slices or smaller wedges. Brush the marzipan with the remaining apricot glaze. Secure the fruits to the cake, alternating the colours.

5 Position the three bundles of cinnamon sticks around the ring. Fill any gaps with the star anise.

▲ *Tie the cinnamon sticks into rough bundles with the fine gold ribbon.*

▲ *Stick the glacé fruits all over the cake, taking care to vary the colours and textures.*

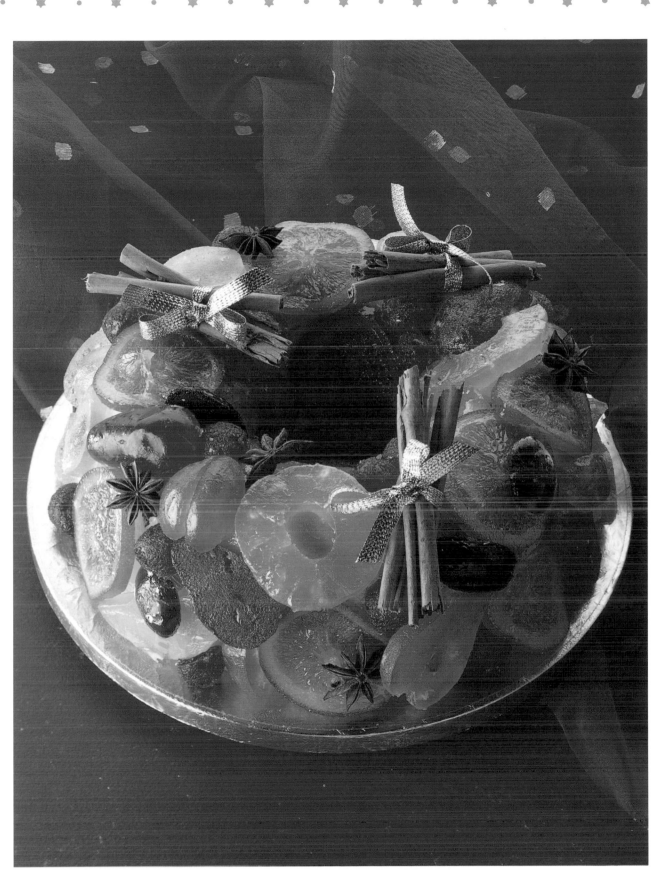

Tiered Christmas Cake

This lavishly decorated centrepiece is achieved by cutting out the centre of a large fruit cake and raising it up to create a two-tier extravaganza.

CAKE AND DECORATION
23cm (9 in) round rich or light fruit cake
90ml (6 tbsp) apricot glaze · 1.5kg (3 lb) marzipan
(almond paste) · 1.5kg (3 lb) sugarpaste · red and
purple food colourings · icing (confectioner's)
sugar and cornflour (cornstarch) for dusting · gold
dusting powder · clear alcohol (gin or vodka)
piping jelly · 2m (2 yd) green paper ribbon
2m (2 yd) red wired ribbon · 125g (4 oz) icing
(confectioner's) sugar · several bunches of bay
leaves · glass tumbler, about 12cm (5 in) tall
6 small gold fir cones · large handful of hazelnuts

EQUIPMENT
13cm (5 in) round flat cake card · 30cm (12 in)
round silver cakeboard · 5cm (2 in) star cutter
fine paintbrush · floristry wire · paper piping bag
dressmaker's pins

1 Place a small tin or saucer measuring 13cm (5 in) in diameter, on top of the fruit cake. Using a knife held upright, cut out the centre of the cake. Carefully ease out and position on the small cake card.

▲ *Place a small tin or saucer on the cake. Cut neatly round it with an upright knife.*

2 Position the outer ring of cake on the board. Brush the cakes with apricot glaze. Roll out 375g (12 oz) of the marzipan and use to cover the smaller cake, easing to fit around the sides and trimming off the excess. Roll out the remaining marzipan to a 30cm (12 in) round. Lay it over the ring cake and ease around the sides to fit. Trim off the excess around the base. Press the marzipan over the central cavity inwards to gauge the inner edge of the cake, then remove the excess with a knife. Re-roll all the trimmings and use to cover the inner sides of the cake.

▲ *Lay the marzipan over the ring cake and ease it into the cavity before trimming the excess.*

▲ *Using the tail-end of a paintbrush, make indentations around the edges of the stars.*

4 To make the gold stars, thinly roll 60g (2 oz) of the white sugarpaste and cut out 10 stars with the cutter. Transfer to a sheet of greaseproof paper. Roll small balls of icing, flatten them slightly then press gently onto the centres of the stars. Using the tail-end of a paintbrush or a skewer, impress holes around the edges of the stars.

5 Paint the centres of the stars with purple food colouring. Mix a little gold dusting powder with clear alcohol until the consistency of thin paint. Use to paint the stars. Once the purple paint has dried, brush with piping jelly to make them shine.

6 To make the ribbon decorations, cut both ribbon types into 25cm (10 in) lengths. Bend in half, then pinch together. Tie with a little floristry wire, twisting well to secure. Bend back the ribbon ends attractively.

3 Reserve 125g (4 oz) of the sugarpaste. Colour the remainder deep red. Roll out 375g (12 oz) of the icing and use to cover the small cake. Roll out the remaining icing and use to cover the large cake, using the same technique as for the marzipan. Use the icing trimmings to cover the cakeboard.

▲ *Bend ribbon in half, then tie with wire to secure loop. Bend back ends.*

TIP
Once assembled, store the cake loosely covered with clingfilm (plastic wrap). If it is to be transported, secure most of the decorations to the larger cake so that the top tier can easily be lifted off.

7 Mix the icing sugar with a little water to make a fairly thin paste. Place in a paper piping bag and snip off the tip. Invert the tumbler into the centre of the large cake then position the small cake over the tumbler. Pipe a little icing onto one of the ribbon ends, then secure to the small cake, if necessary supporting with a pin until

◀ *If necessary, pin the ribbon to the small cake until the icing hardens. Add more ribbons and bay leaves to hide the tumbler.*

the icing hardens a little. Secure more ribbons and bay leaves between the two tiers and over the top of the cake.

8 Secure the fir cones and nuts in the same way, filling in the gaps between the ribbons. Arrange the gold stars in prominent positions, allowing room for the tassels to hang down. For each tassel, very thinly roll a little white sugarpaste to a 4cm (1½ in) square.

Using a fine-bladed knife, make cuts along the square, leaving the icing intact at one side. Lightly dampen the uncut area of icing then roll up the tassel, and cut off the excess uncut area.

9 Roll small balls of icing and secure with the tassels to the points of the stars. Leave to harden. Use a little more of the dusting powder and alcohol to paint the tassels with a fine brush.

▼ *To make tassels, cut squares of thin paste, make cuts on one side, then roll up from the top.*

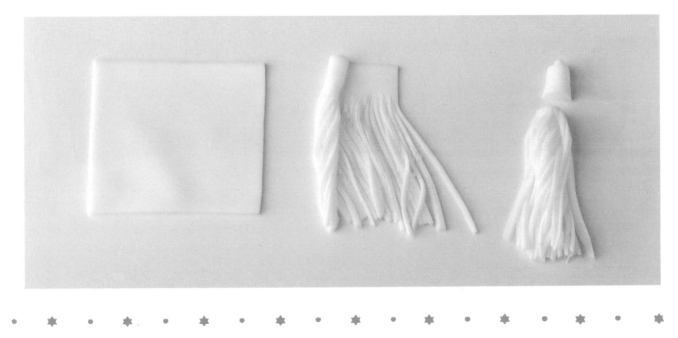

Christmas Rose Cake

A ring of Christmas roses and rich collar of festive ribbon transforms a simple royal-iced cake into something special.

CAKE AND DECORATION

20cm (8 in) round rich or light fruit cake
45ml (3 tbsp) apricot glaze · 1kg (2 lb) marzipan
(almond paste) · 125g (4 oz) sugarpaste, optional
triple quantity royal icing · 50g (2 oz) bought
petal paste · yellow dusting powder · white
stamens · 0.75m (28 in) firm gold ribbon, about
5cm (2½ in) wide · 2m (2 yd) fine green or red
wired ribbon · 1m (1 yd) fine ribbon for
board edge

EQUIPMENT

28cm (11 in) round gold cakeboard · palette knife
foil · medium rose petal cutter · cocktail sticks
(toothpicks) · piece of foam sponge · soft
paintbrush · paper piping bag

1 Brush the cake with apricot glaze and cover with marzipan. Place on the cakeboard. Cover the edges of the board with the sugarpaste if liked. Reserve 60ml (4 tbsp) of the royal icing. Spread the remainder over the top and sides of the cake until covered in one even layer. Work the palette knife around the sides of the cake, then over the top to neaten. Leave to set.

2 To make the Christmas roses, roll some strips of foil, then shape into rounds about 5cm (2 in) in diameter. Place on a sheet of greaseproof paper. You will need 11 altogether, allowing one spare. Take a little petal paste and roll as thinly as possible. Cut out five petals with the cutter. Roll a cocktail stick over the edges of the petal to give a delicate, lightly curled edge. Press each petal onto a piece of sponge to lightly cup it.

▲ *Cover the cake with royal icing and work the palette knife around it.*

▲ *Cut out the petals, then roll the edges with a cocktail stick to lift and curl them.*

3 Lightly dampen one side of each of the five petals. Arrange the petals, slightly overlapping, inside a foil ring so that the rose is supported by the foil. Make the remaining roses in the

same way and leave to harden for 24 hours.

4 Using the soft brush, lightly colour the centre of each rose with dusting powder. Place the reserved royal icing in the piping bag and snip off the tip. Pipe a dot of icing into the centre of a rose. Cut about a dozen stamens down to 1cm (½ in) depth and press several at a time into the royal icing. Finish the remainder in the same way.

5 Secure the roses in a ring around the edge of the cake with a dot of royal icing. Tie the firm gold ribbon around the cake and secure with a dot of icing. Loosely pleat the wired ribbon concertina-fashion between the fingers and thumbs. Secure over the gold ribbon. Secure the ribbon around the top edge of the board.

▲ *Lightly dampen one side of each petal and arrange them, slightly overlapping, inside a foil ring.*

▶ *Pipe a dot of icing into each rose centre, then add a dozen stamens, a few at a time.*

TIP

If more convenient, sugarpaste can be used instead of the petal paste to make the roses. However, the results will not be quite as delicate.

White Ivy Cake

Generously 'embroidered' with a pretty selection of leaves, and trimmed with pearls, this festive cake is both classic and stylish.

CAKE AND DECORATION

25 x 20cm (10 x 8 in) oval rich or light fruit cake, made using mixture for a 23cm (9 in) round tin
45ml (3 tbsp) apricot glaze · 1kg (2 lb) marzipan (almond paste) · 1.5kg (3 lb) sugarpaste · icing (confectioner's) sugar and cornflour (cornstarch) for dusting · 1 quantity royal icing · 45cm (18 in) pearlized beading for top of cake · 1m (1 yd) pearlized beading for base of cake · pearlized white dusting powder · clear alcohol (gin or vodka) · white candles · 1m (1 yd) ribbon for board edge

EQUIPMENT

30 x 25cm (12 x 10 in) oval silver cakeboard greaseproof paper · dressmaker's pins · paper piping bags · fine writing tube (tip) · small, medium and large ivy leaf cutters · medium and large holly cutters · leaf veiner · fine paintbrush

---

1 Brush the cake with apricot glaze and cover with marzipan (almond paste). Place on the cakeboard. Reserve 500g (1 lb) of the sugarpaste. Use the remainder to cover the cake. Use a little more icing to cover the cakeboard around the base of the cake.

2 Draw an oval template measuring 15 x 10cm (6 x 4 in) onto a piece of greaseproof paper and cut it out. Lay it on the centre of the cake and mark the outline with a pin. Beat the royal icing, adding a little water or lemon juice until it is softly peaking. Place in the piping bag fitted with the writing tube. Trim the beading for the top of the cake so that it fits neatly over the marked line. Press it gently down, securing the ends with a dot of icing. Arrange the beading around the cake sides, securing the ends as above.

3 Roll out a little of the sugarpaste and cut out ivy and holly leaves in various sizes. Mark each with a veiner or knife then secure to the cake, bunching two or three holly leaves together and graduating the strings of ivy leaves from small to large.

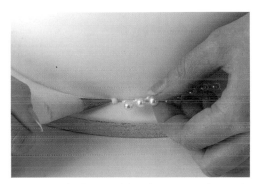

▲ *Attach the pearl beading to the base of the cake, securing it with a dot of icing.*

▲ *Attach the leaves, grouping the holly together and graduating the size of the ivy.*

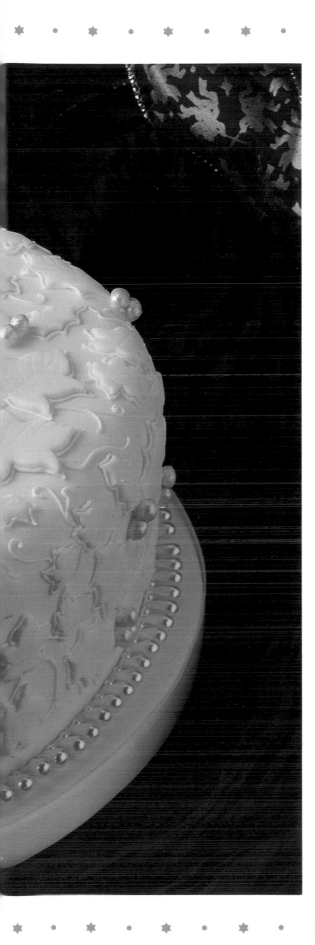

4 Pipe a fine outline around all the leaves, then add decorative trails of icing around the ivy leaves, particularly where there are large gaps between them.

5 Roll small balls of sugarpaste to represent holly berries and secure with a little icing to the holly leaves. Mix a little of the dusting powder with enough clear alcohol to give the consistency of thin paint. Use to paint over the holly berries. Gently press the white candles into the top of the cake. Secure the ribbon around the edge of the board.

TIP

If you do not have an oval cake tin, and cannot hire one from a cake-decorating shop, this cake can be made equally successfully using a 23cm (9 in) round cake tin. Use a 12cm (5 in) circle to mark the position for the heading on top of the cake.

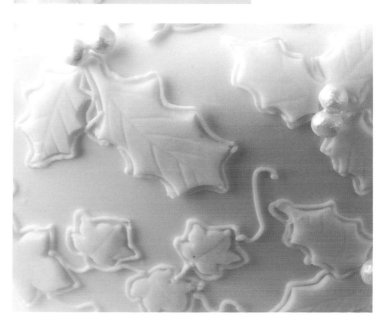

◀ *Pipe an outline around the leaves, adding loops and trails around the ivy to link them.*

▼ *Add balls of white paste to represent holly berries.*

Templates

The templates shown here are actual size, and can be reduced or enlarged on a photocopier.

ANGEL

CHRISTMAS STORYBOOKS
Page 48

SANTA COMES TO TOWN
Page 23

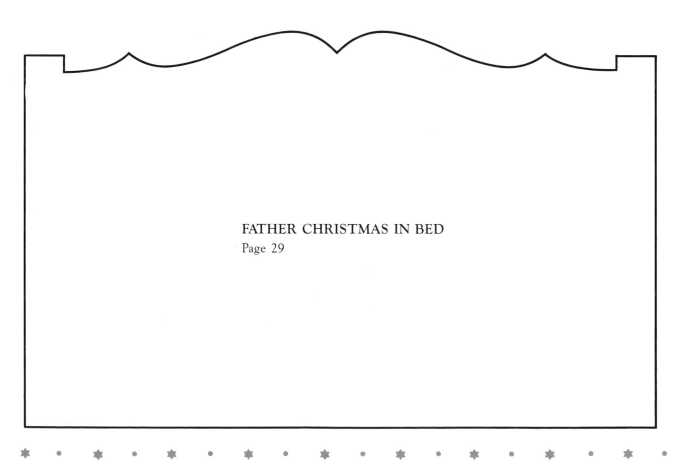

FATHER CHRISTMAS IN BED
Page 29

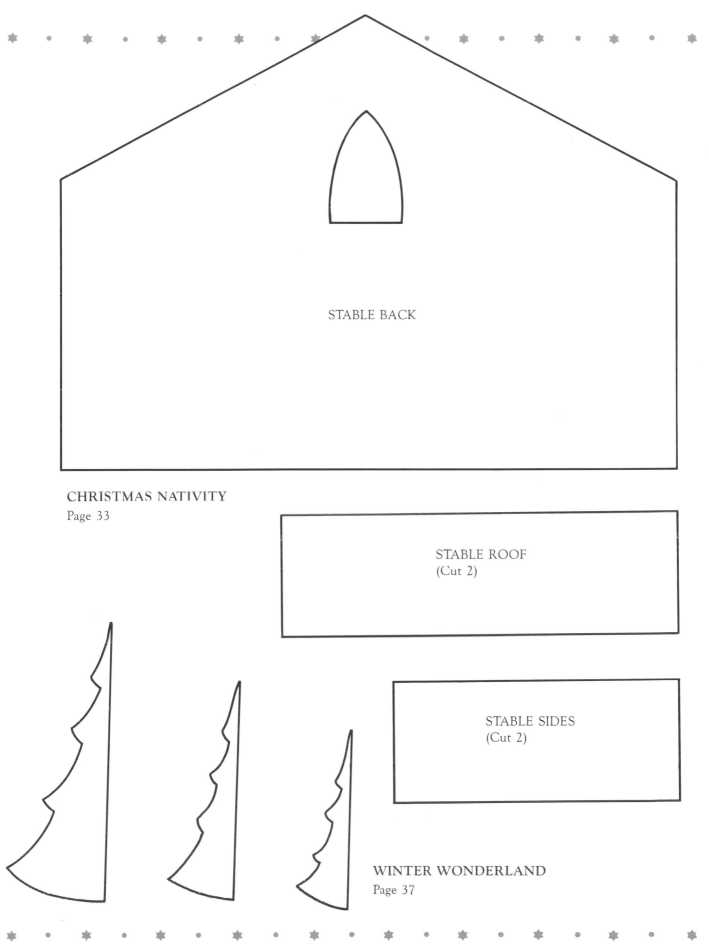

STABLE BACK

CHRISTMAS NATIVITY
Page 33

STABLE ROOF
(Cut 2)

STABLE SIDES
(Cut 2)

WINTER WONDERLAND
Page 37

Index

Acknowledgements

The publishers would like thank the
following suppliers:

Cake Art Ltd
Venture Way,
Crown Estate,
Priorswood,
Taunton, TA2 8DE

Guy, Paul and Co. Ltd
Unit B4,
Foundry Way,
Little End Road,
Eaton Socon,
Cambs, PE19 3JH

Squires Kitchen
Squires House,
3 Waverley Lane,
Farnham,
Surrey, GU9 8BB

Anniversary House
(Cake Decorations) Ltd
Unit 16,
Elliott Road,
West Howe Industrial Estate,
Bournemouth, BH11 8LZ